JEFF BEZOS:

AN EXTRAORDINARY LIFE

MARK SMITH

Table of Contents

Introduction

Chapter 1 - A Moon Shot: Jeff Bezos' Boyhood

Chapter 2 - Bezos Bootstraps: The Challenges & Struggles of Founding Amazon

Chapter 3 - Jeff Bezos: Little Known Facts

Chapter 4 - The Tactics and Techniques

    Think Long Term:

    Self-Improvement:

    Life Long Reader:

    Be Kind:

    Be Humble:

    Think Around Problems:

    Hire Well:

    Have Very High Standards:

    Work Ethic:

    Family Support is Key:

    Focus On Your Passions:

Chapter 5 - 20 Pieces of Advice for Lasting Success

Chapter 6 - Make It So: Jeff Bezos' Philanthropic Life

Conclusion: The Life of Jeff Bezos

Copyright © 2019 Mark Smith

All rights reserved. No part of this book may be reproduced or transmitted in any form or by any means, electronic or mechanical, including photocopying, recording or by any information storage and retrieval system without written permission of the publisher, except for the inclusion of brief quotations in a review.

Introduction

"When you are 80 years old, and in a quiet moment of reflection only for yourself in the most personal version of your life story, the telling that will be the most compact and meaningful will be a series of choices you have made. In the end, we are our choices."

— Jeff Bezos

Jeff Bezos believes in taking calculated risks — and he's reaped the rewards. He is the founder and CEO of Amazon, the wealthiest man in modern history, routinely makes lists of the earth's most influential leaders, and is currently developing space tech with the far-reaching ambition of space colonization. However, it would have taken great foresight to have predicted that Jeff would achieve any of these things: he was born to a high school student and was raised in a blended family without much money.

Despite an untraditional start, Jeff flourished at Princeton and then on Wall Street. However, he was fascinated by what was considered by many to be a passing nineties era fad — *the internet*. At great personal risk, Jeff quit his position as a senior vice president with a six-figure income and left with his new wife for Seattle. He was going to sell online books. As he struggled to make his vision for e-commerce a reality, he faced down the Dotcom bust, saw millions of dollars in lost profits, withstood vicious competitors, and weathered thousands of failed ventures.

For Jeff, all the struggle and the loss were worth it— Because in the end... we are our choices.

There are plenty of books on this subject on the market, thanks again for choosing this one! Every effort was made to ensure it is full of as much useful information as possible; please enjoy!

Chapter 1 - A Moon Shot: Jeff Bezos' Boyhood

In mid-July of 1969, the United States and the rest of the world watched breathlessly as Neil Armstrong became the first human being to break the powdery surface of the moon. Armstrong's quip, "One small step for man; one giant leap for mankind," reverberated across the earth as his footprints marked the first major victory in the global space race. 238,900 miles away from the Apollo mission, a five-year-old boy sat watching his television, spellbound, in the heat of a New Mexico Summer. This kindergartener would be forever ignited by this fateful evening's broadcast to carry on Armstrong's torch in the space race. In pursuit of this relay, Jeff Bezos would become the wealthiest man in modern history, lead the greatest progress in book publishing since Gutenberg invented the printing press almost five hundred years before, and as the founder of Amazon, shake the world's economy in ways unseen since the Industrial Revolution. Jeff Bezos would later say that you do not find your passions, your passions find you — in that fateful moonwalk, Neil Armstrong's accomplishment found, and energized the young boy in a way that would resound as much through history as Armstrong's first giant leap on the moon for mankind.

This titan of industry was born Jeffrey Preston Jorgenson, January 12, 1964, to his seventeen-year-old mother Jackie Jorgenson while she was still in high school. Jackie was married to eighteen-year-old unicyclist Ted Jorgenson who belonged to a circus troupe and is believed to have struggled with drinking. Jorgenson has been described as a deadbeat father and husband, and as a teen mother, Jackie was ostracized by the community for her pregnancy. Reportedly, the school tried to have her expelled, but her father rose to the occasion and defended Jackie.

During Jeff's babyhood, his parents struggled over money issues. Ted Jorgenson was making $1.25 an hour with his troupe, and the couple struggled financially. After less than two years, the couple split over economic hardship. Ted Jorgenson would never see his son again. Years later, a reporter tracked down a 69-year-old Jorgenson to interview him about Jeff. Jorgenson said he wasn't even aware that his son was alive. The reporter said he seemed confused at being approached with information about his son— he was shocked to find out that Jeff had grown up to be the famous founder of Amazon, Jeff Bezos. Jorgenson said he had a phone number for Jeff and his mother, but it had seemed best to him to keep at a distance. He would admit that he had not been a good father to his son.

The early prelude to Jeff Bezos life was not promising, but his mother Jackie remarried— she wed Miguel "Mike" Bezos when Jeff was four years old. He adopted Jeff as his son, and Jeff's name was changed from Jorgenson to Jeff Bezos. Mike's example as a father would help to instill work ethic and drive in his son: Mike Bezos was a refugee from Cuba who had come alone to the United States. At the time of his immigration, he only spoke one word of English, "hamburger." Mike was an extremely dedicated worker: he learned English as a teenager at a Jesuit mission. With a scholarship and odd jobs, he put himself through school in New Mexico to become an engineer with Exxon, where he would work for thirty years.

Jeff demonstrated early independence and ingenuity: at three years old he took his crib apart with a screwdriver because he thought it was time; he had a grown-up bed. His family, instead of being cross, were encouraging toward Jeff's mechanical genius. As a boy, Jeff's room became cluttered with his inventions, parts, and experiments. Jeff's two younger siblings, Mark and Christine, who were very young at the time, thought his work equated to great toys to play with. So, Jeff invented an alarm system that would trigger with a loud buzzing sound when they entered his bedroom. After Jeff's room became too filled with his projects, his parents surrendered their garage to become his invention space. Calling himself a "garage inventor," Jeff developed a myriad of ingenious creations: He designed a solar heater out of an umbrella and tin foil, created amateur robots, and experimented with developing electronics. He spent time making a gate that closed automatically with old tires. He even worked on a hovercraft that he adapted from parts of the family vacuum cleaner.

The family moved to Texas when Jeff was in the fourth grade. He spent a great deal of time with his grandfather Lawrence Preston "Pop." Jeff's Pop was descended from early settlers of Texas and had inherited a 25,000-acre farm. His grandfather had been the regional director of the U.S. Atomic Energy Commission and oversaw Los Alamos and Lawrence Livermore nuclear laboratories, but he took an early retirement to spend time working his vast family ranch. Growing up, Jeff spent an enormous amount of time with his grandparents on the farm. Pop greatly indulged Jeff's taste for robotics and mechanical toys. His grandfather's elite background in science was very shaping for the young boy. Jeff did a vast number of chores, spending time with his grandfather on the ranch, called the "Lazy G" — they did their own veterinary work vaccinating cows, laying down pipe, working on windmills, and performing electrical work. Charmingly, they watched soap operas together every afternoon; they never missed episodes of *Days of Our Lives*. U.S. society may have lost some of its hometown, agrarian roots, but Jeff was getting the true Americana experience. Jeff's world was also widened and influenced by getting to occasionally go on road trips with his grandparents. They owned an airstream, which is an R.V. that looks something like a Twinkie made out aluminum. Jeff remembers that he worshipped spending time with his grandparents and loved experiencing their airstream club called the Caravan Club. This involved hundreds of airstreams in a row exploring U.S. highways all the way up through Canada.

Jeff showed an early aptitude with computers. He began working with them in the fourth grade: His school offered teletype machines and a local business donated time on their computers to students. A few boys, including Jeff, took advantage of the offer. They used their computer time to teach themselves to code using books and to play computerized *Star Trek* games.

As a boy, Jeff enjoyed reading science fiction— he had an early appreciation for J.R.R. Tolkien's *Hobbit* and especially liked anything about space exploration. He amused his teachers with his fascination with conquering the frontier of space: he told them he wanted to be an astronaut and space entrepreneur when he grew up. One of his mother Jackie's favorite stories was a space-themed speech he gave that she still keeps. Adorably, Jeff's speech opens with the *Star Trek* line, "space the final frontier." It went on to detail his plan to have humanity move off of the planet, with earth reverting to a nature preserve. He thought humanity was banking too much on having earth for a home and needed to explore other options. When asked about this speech as an adult, Jeff smirked a little, but he grew serious when he said we definitely have all of our eggs in one basket.

At ten years old, Jeff was told for the first time that he was adopted by his step-father. Reflecting as an adult, Jeff said that he had been more fazed at that age by learning that he was going to have to start wearing glasses, than by the revelation. This pragmatic attitude that Jeff adopted even as a child was something he would carry with him into adulthood. As an adult discussing his biological father, Jeff said simply that as far as he was concerned his stepdad (Mike) is his real dad. He continued that the only time that he thought about his biological father was when he was filling out medical forms. Jeff's deep commitment to family and their support is what he attributes much of his success to. He has been quoted as telling his mother that he won the lottery with her — that he owes her everything. Jeff believes that the secret of his ability to be a risk taker is having a great support system at home. He reflected on his dad Mike's time in a Jesuit camp for recent immigrant children: "My dad, who's a Cuban immigrant ... he came to the US when he was sixteen in a refugee camp in the Everglades," Jeff continued that, "(My family) is so loving and supportive." He says that when you have loving people in your life like, "(his wife) MacKenzie, my parents, my grandfather, my grandmother — you end up being able to take risks. Because I think it's one of those things, you know, you kind of know that somebody's got your back — And so if you're thinking about it logically — it's an emotional thing." It's very Jeff to approach even the logistics of emotional support in a logical way, but the sentiment is clear: he is grateful to have had a family support system to achieve his goals.

After their move to Texas, Jeff's parents were concerned that Jeff wasn't adapting to school as well as they would like and decided to put him into football. They thought a team sport would aid his ability to make friends. Jeff was a scrawny kid to be joining the fast-paced, competitive world of football in Houston, Texas. His mother Jackie remembers that he was so small that Jeff was barely was able to make the required weight to join the team, and she was afraid that he was going, "get creamed," while he was out playing. Jeff was poor at throwing even a baseball; it was said that: "His aim proved so unpredictable that his mother tied a mattress to the fence and asked him to practice on his own." However, Jeff used his capacity for problem-solving to succeed in the game. His coach gave him the position of defensive captain after only two weeks of playing: Jeff could remember the plays and where all the kids were supposed to be on the field in a way that most of the other players couldn't.

Jeff remembers that he was, "dead set against playing football. I had no interest in playing a game where people would tackle me to the ground." However, Jeff revealed his characteristically fearsome competitive streak as he played. And despite his initial reluctance to join the team, when they lost the league championship, he was moved to tears.

Jeff was enrolled in the Vanguard school program, which was designed for gifted students. He excelled at the out-of-the-box thought lines that his teachers encouraged. Jeff was a highly competitive scholar, and his ingenuity could border cheekiness. As part of a project for his sixth-grade math class, he developed a system of grading teachers in his school to graph their performance. He garnered, calculated, and graphed the resulting poll data. He asserted the survey he had developed and given to his fellow students wasn't a teacher popularity contest; the polling would determine their acumen as teachers.

Jeff demonstrated an early, fierce commitment to thinking independently. In one Vanguard school discussion, Jeff remarked to a fellow sixth grader that, "The way the world is, you know, someone could tell you to press the button. You have to be able to think what you're doing for yourself." One teacher said of Jeff that, "There is probably no limit to what he can do, given a little guidance." However, although his teachers scored him as a confident student, they believed he possessed a low potential for leadership skills.

The Bezos family moved to Miami, Florida when Jeff was a teenager. In high school, Jeff was an excellent student: he maintained straight A's. He participated in the University of Florida's Student Science Training Program. He was a National Merit Scholar and received the Silver Knight Award, which Jeff remembers as the first formal recognition of his academic excellence. One fellow student remembers that when Jeff announced that he was competing to become the class valedictorian the other students knew that they were now competing for second place. Jeff achieved valedictorian, and in his speech, he spoke about his desire to take humanity off planet. Jeff told the *Miami Herald* that he wanted to "build space hotels, amusement parks, yachts and colonies for two or three million people orbiting around the earth." Another student recounts that despite the scope of his vision, Jeff was a deeply grounded human being even in high school.

In school, Jeff's life was surreally down to earth: he took a job working the breakfast shift at McDonald's. Jeff laughed that, "They wouldn't let me anywhere near the customers. This was my acned-teenager stage. They were like, 'Hmm, why don't you work in the back?' Chuckling he continued that, "One of the great gifts I got from that job is that I can crack eggs with one hand."

He was fascinated by the mechanical efficiency of McDonald's, but the nature of the work motivated him the following Summer to found his first business venture: The Dream Institute. Fifth and sixth-grade students were invited to enroll for six hundred dollars. The Dream Institute was a camp that emphasized science and the classics. Jeff advertised that using classics like *Gulliver's Travels, The Lord of the Rings*, and exploring scientific subjects like black holes and electronics, prepared students for critical thinking later in life. He enrolled six students to his institute. His emphasis on critical thinking would follow Jeff throughout his professional career — dictating hiring choices and company policy.

His high school girlfriend Ursula Werner helped him co-found the camp. She remembers that even at that time Jeff was interested in making a lot of money, but she says that it wasn't about becoming wealthy. He wanted to be able to do great things, shape the future for humanity in a real way. Growing up, Jeff's heroes were Thomas Edison, Stephen Hawking, and Walt Disney. As a young inventor himself, Jeff found Thomas Edison, as one of the nation's great inventor's, to be a source of boyhood inspiration. Likewise, Jeff found Disney's development of mechanics to be fascinating. Mechanical wonder rides like Disney's Pirates of the Caribbean, Space Mountain, and Starcade all opened during Jeff's childhood. However, it was the scope of Disney's vision that Jeff truly found inspiring. He remembered that Disney had to convince investors to contribute 400 million dollars to his venture. Jeff must have sympathized with Disney's vision of the future, and his according need to engage and catalyze others to make it succeed. Jeff found the capacity to see what seemed like fancy, become reality. Disney's motto, "keep moving forward," must also have appealed to Jeff's inventive, adaptive nature.

Following high school, in 1982, Jeff received early admittance into Princeton, where it was his ambition to follow in his hero Stephen Hawking's footsteps. He would later say that he chose Princeton specifically to have the opportunity to study physics. Accordingly, Jeff pursued classes in theoretical physics, but he soon felt that he was deficient in the ability to operate as a top-level physicist— In characteristically self-deprecating humor he remembers feeling that there were two or three other real geniuses in his physics class, and he wasn't keeping up in the same way. Jeff said that in theoretical physics if you weren't leading the way you were merely trying to keep up with those that were, and even at that age Jeff Bezos wasn't ready to stand on anyone else's shoulders. He switched to study computer science and electrical engineering.

While at Princeton, Jeff was introduced in a class to the concept of the internet for the first time. However, he wouldn't think about its commercial potential for several years to come. Jeff continued with his love affair with space quest: he served as President of the Princeton chapter of the Students for the Exploration and Development of Space. He connected with professors that were involved in advocating for and developing the theory of space colonization — including Professor Gerard O'Neill. O'Neill theorized that space colonization was superior to earth as a platform for an expanding tech civilization, which must have sparked with the space-colony-ambitious Jeff.

In 1986, Jeff graduated from Princeton with highest honors: Phi Beta Kappa and Tau Beta Pi. Jeff Bezos was all grown up. He stood at five foot eight and weighed one hundred and fifty-four pounds — the features of his face had rounded, and his dark eyes would crinkle when he smiled — which was often. His sandy hair was already beginning to get a little thin, but those that met him described him as a cheerful, upbeat man with an impressive intellect. Alternately kind and alarmingly intense, Jeff's most iconic feature was to become his unusual, machine gun-style laugh. This defining laugh was so distinctive that it produced polarizing reactions. It helped woo the woman that would eventually become his wife, but also reportedly offset his ability to negotiate with some competitors. When asked about his laugh Jeff took a self-effacing, humorous approach, remarking that, "Well, I come from a long line of goofy people." As an adult, he emphasized healthy eating but developed a passion for unusual foods and food truck vendors. Reportedly, at one meeting, he ordered breakfast octopus — he said even with food he is just looking to try the thing that he doesn't understand.

After graduation, Jeff was seduced by top computer companies from around the world: Intel, Bell Labs, and Anderson Consulting all pursued him as a candidate. However, Jeff chose to work at a startup: Fitel. He worked successfully for the new company to debug lines of code. His success drove him up in the company, where he landed a position as the head of development and director of customer service. This telecommunications business called to his entrepreneurial spirit, but he didn't stay with the company for very long. Like many driven, vision-oriented individuals he accepted challenges but needed constant change to be professionally satisfied.

Following Intel, Jeff worked at Banker's Trust, where he created and improved systems for investment. Once more, his prowess caused him to excel at the company, and he was given a position as vice president at Banker's. After two years, Jeff was ready for the axis of his career to turn once more. He rotated back toward his early passion for tech. Jeff accepted a job at the age of 26 with the hedge company D.E. Shaw.

Jeff found his partner, while he was working at D.E. Shaw. He met his future wife Mackenzie who was working at Shaw as a researcher at the time. She was also a Princeton alum just like Jeff, who said he was primarily looking to be with someone resourceful— She was a very bright woman that had worked as an assistant with author Toni Morrison in college. They did not experience immediate attraction. Rather, Mackenzie and Jeff fell in love over time— Mackenzie would later say that Jeff was her opposite; he is outgoing, fearless with strangers. He is charming at cocktail parties, while she is rather shy. Ultimately, it was his laugh that won her over: she would hear it throughout the office and wonder who could resist that laugh? She tells people that if Jeff's not happy, just wait five minutes.

Outsiders talked about how the couple fell in love in group settings — slowly, but when they fell for each other, it became obvious to everyone around them. Jeff had finally found his resourceful woman. What he didn't know was that he had also found a partner that would take a professional blind leap with him just eighteen months later. One D.E. Shaw associate remembered that Jeff had rented a limousine to treat the firm's associates to a night out but that Jeff's clear intention was to pursue Mackenzie. However, Mackenzie claims that she was actually the one to make the initial move toward a relationship, she asked Jeff out to lunch. Jeff has described his romance with Mackenzie as a very "*Ally McBeal* sort of romance." After just three months of dating, they decided to become engaged. Jeff and Mackenzie married after a short three-month engagement in 1993.

Their partnership provided an important level of stability for Jeff and the four children that he and Mackenzie would later raise together. As always, family was of terrific importance to Jeff, and Mackenzie drove him to work until 2013 before dropping off their children at school. They had three sons and an adopted daughter from China. The children have a five-year age range.

Reportedly, Jeff tells his children that they need to be proud of their choices, not of their talents. Jeff tells them that you can be happy about the way that you look or about being handsome, but what defines you is what you choose to do with your life— one of the choices Jeff has made as a father is to invest time in his children: The family always sat down to a healthy breakfast, and Jeff prioritized them by not scheduling early morning meetings at Amazon as a rule. MacKenzie was quoted as saying the couple had tried many things with their four children— Including that they had experimented with homeschooling them. Mackenzie said that they had tried, "off-season travel, kitchen-science experiments, chicken incubation, Mandarin lessons (logical, considering that they adopted their daughter from China)… she continued, "the Singapore math program, and lots of clubs and sports with other neighborhood kids."

Mackenzie worked on books, becoming an author in her own right, eventually. She warmly noted that Jeff is her very best reader. Despite his numerous engagements, even when Amazon became staggeringly successful, Jeff would lay down projects to read Mackenzie's latest work. Jeff also loved to surprise Mackenzie with clothes—- Jeff said that "Sometimes I call her and say, 'What's your such-and-such size?' and she says, 'Why?' and I say, 'None of your business!'" She was delighted by Jeff's impetuous surprises. Jeff also ended each day by doing the dishes, laughing that it is probably the sexiest thing that he does. In an interview featuring eleven factors describing Jeff Bezos, his wife comes first is the final descriptor. When describing Jeff's feelings for Mackenzie, it was said that: "The man loves to play hardball, but when it comes to his wife, Jeff turns into a romantic. He loves to pamper his wife and would cancel all his appointments for the day to read her manuscripts. Reportedly, Bezos love to buy presents for his wife and constantly tends to surprise her. Jeff recommends it to every man. They have been described as an almost unnaturally close-knit family, which is something to wonder at considering the grueling hours and pressures that Jeff and Mackenzie inevitably faced with the challenges of the genesis of Amazon.

At D.E. Shaw, Jeff once more achieved professional success and rose through the company's ranks. He became the youngest vice president in the company's history, and within four years he gained the title of senior vice president of the company. Its founder, Shaw, was instrumental in Jeff's interest in the future of online commerce — they had meetings where they attempted to project and develop the concepts that would transform this new market space. With Shaw's shared interest in this internet experiment lab, Jeff had the opportunity to explore early internet trends and investigate them. During these meetings, Jeff and Shaw had almost supernatural foresight into e-commerce avenues that would eventually succeed. They imagined precursor programs that would eventually look like Gmail and E-trade. They even had an exchange where they discussed the concept of an "everything store." Later in a biography of Jeff's success with Amazon, it was shared that, "Shaw himself confirmed the internet-store concept… he told the *New York Times Magazine,* "The idea was always that someone would be allowed to make a profit as an intermediary;" he continued, "the key question is, who will get to be that middleman?"

However, in 1994, at the age of thirty, one chance news article changed the course of Jeff's life, and the global economy forever. He read that the internet had experienced a 2,300 percent growth in one year. The statistic consumed him. He foresaw that even this staggering growth in internet commerce was a marketplace in its infancy. He wanted to get in on the ground floor of this tech boom.

Jeff began to do tremendous research about online businesses. He made a list of avenues that had the potential to burgeon as e-commerce markets. Eventually, he narrowed his list down to twenty investment candidates, but he settled on pursuing online book sales. He was animated at the idea of a selection of millions of works. It was a store that could never physically exist, but an online presence would make it possible. That night, Jeff hosted a party in his upscale New York apartment; they were enjoying the final installment of *Star Trek: The Next Generation*. And the very next day, he was on a plane from New York to Los Angeles to attend a book seller's convention. He came back convinced that he could make a success of an online book store; it would be a step toward his future of the "everything store."

Jeff remembered in one interview: "Our timing was good, our choice of product categories (books) was a very good choice;" Jeff continued that, "And we did a lot of analysis on that to pick that category as the first best category for E-commerce online, but there were no guarantees that that was a good category," And Jeff recalled the economic climate. "At the time we launched this business it wasn't even crystal clear that the technology would improve fast enough that ordinary people… (people unfamiliar with online purchasing) would even want to bother with this technology. Jeff remembered his pick of an online book store as very good luck.

Initially, Jeff tried to get D.E. Shaw in on the campaign, but the company wasn't in a place to invest. However, he realized that if he didn't pursue his ambitions with the online book store, he would always regret the loss — even more than if he failed at his venture. To complicate matters, Mackenzie and Jeff had only been married a single year; his job with the hedge fund was very secure, with excellent pay. He remembers that he had a great boss in Shaw and liked his colleagues. It was a tremendous risk to quit and gamble on an almost wholly untested market. After Jeff shared his ambitions to start an online book store, Mackenzie said she would back him up if he wanted to quit.

Jeff approached his boss, Shaw, to tell him that he was planning to quit to start an online book business. With their collaboration over the future of internet commerce, it could not have come as a shock to Shaw that Jeff wanted to pursue one of these entrepreneurial avenues. Shaw himself had decided as a younger man to spend time on Wall Street before he entered the internet commerce race. Kindly, concerned about Jeff's security, Shaw asked Jeff to take a walk with him through New York City's Central Park. They walked, discussing Jeff's ambitions for over two hours. Jeff remembers that Shaw told him it sounded like a very good opportunity... but it would be a better opportunity for someone that didn't already have such a good job— and with a true competitor's spirit, Shaw also told Jeff that D.E. Shaw's ventures might compete with Jeff's new startup. Shaw's gentle, cautionary words shook Jeff and his initial fearless joy about pursuing this new venture. Shaw convinced Jeff on their walk to take 48 hours to think about his decision.

Nevertheless, Jeff was terrified of being haunted by what might have been, the things he might have accomplished if he had tried. Jeff knew that he wouldn't enjoy failure, but ignoring his ambitions was intolerable. He would one day declare that: "If you decide that you're going to do only the things you know are going to work — you're going to leave a lot of opportunity on the table."

48 hours after his conversation with Shaw, Jeff had made his globe-altering-life-risk. He quit.

Chapter 2 - Bezos Bootstraps: The Challenges & Struggles of Founding Amazon

Mackenzie and Jeff sat staring, watching the dawn rise over the edge of one of the wonders of the United States. It was July of 1994 and the heat of the desert day was just beginning. The Bezos couple were in awe as the sun crept over the beauty of the Grand Canyon rim. They had taken time out of what would become a legendary road trip to enjoy its scenic, famed beauty.

The couple was also figuratively looking out over the edge. Jeff Bezos had quit his secure position as a senior vice president with D.E. Shaw to start his online book business endeavor. Recently, the couple had flown down to Texas to borrow Jeff's grandfather's car. His grandfather Preston was there for Jeff once more, he lent the young couple his beat up 1988 Chevy Blazer to make their road trip. They needed the car to make the long three-thousand-mile trek from their home in New York City to Seattle. It was official— like so many other American pioneers, Jeff and Mackenzie were leaving the East Coast to settle out West and make their fortunes. Like true pioneers, that trip out West was not a deeply glamorous experience. On one night, they rattled up to the Rambler motel, which was so dirty that Mackenzie refused to remove her shoes.

Nonetheless, the couple could not fail to appreciate the United States' beauty. Their moment's repose overlooking the Grand Canyon, watching the dawning over the canyon. it was just a lovely detour on their journey to the rising ambition of Jeff's dream that would someday become Amazon.

Jeff's success was a very American tale: he is a self-starter, a man of bootstrap caliber. He was born the son of a teenage high school student who raised him with his Cuban immigrant step-father. They parented a boy that would go on to be an Ivy League graduate, succeeding at the top of New York City's Wall Street game. They also raised a tech pioneer, capable of great risk. After all, he left an estimated six-figure salary and handsome bonus; together with his new wife and their dog Kamala (a space enthusiast to the last, Kamala was named after an obscure character from Star Trek). In further reference to the American call to ingenuity, Jeff was now embarking on a cross-country road trip that spanned only a fraction of the global empire that he would conquer with his start-up.

During the trip, Mackenzie drove, while Jeff made plans for his new enterprise. From the passenger seat, he sat clicking furiously away at his laptop. He made business projections and called investors, trying to get set up and secure seed money to begin work on his new project. His goal, he remembers, was to build not just a valuable company, but one that would last. Most of Jeff's projections from the trip would turn out to be wrong— Amazon became wildly more successful than even his broad, literal reach for the stars could have led him to hope for. But in the beginning, this venture was nothing more than a risky experiment that had its moments of fear and desperation.

Jeff had selected Seattle as a headquarters for several reasons: Ingrams was there; it was a wholesale book seller he would have close access to. At the time there were only two in the nation, so, Jeff's options were somewhat restricted in terms of the physical locale for his book business. He also knew that the city provided a very high level of tech talent for him to choose from the candidate pool. Operating from Seattle also meant that he would initially only be selling to the surrounding Washington state residents, which was a relatively small population. Jeff considered the smaller population of the state to be a bonus because it meant that he could avoid the hefty sales tax that a more populace state would entail.

Mackenzie and Jeff made it to Seattle and began setting up their new two-bedroom home. Jeff would use the garage of their new home as his workspace. He was back to his childhood roots, working as a "garage inventor." They ran a series of extension cords that webbed through the garage to power the place. The drafty, poorly insulated garage was heated with a potbellied stove that sat in the middle of the room. Jeff, ever pragmatic and careful with their very tight funds, built his own desks and work tables — saving money further by using doors he bought at the Home Depot. The entire setup for each desk cost under sixty dollars. To this day, desks for employees at Amazon use this door-craft model; in spite of his success, Jeff has never lost his roots. In celebration of Amazon's innovative, frugal roots, employees win the "Door Desk Awards" when they have a particularly brilliant or insightful professional moment. Jeff calls it a, "well built moment."

When Jeff arrived in Seattle the next phase in developing his startup was looking for his very first employee. Jeff's hiring model was developed during this phase: he always sought to make every new hire an improvement to the current talent pool. In later years, Jeff would become famous for his obsessive hiring strategy. He would often grill interviewers about their meetings with candidates. He would use their feedback to construct elaborate, scrawling whiteboard charts of the pros and cons of possible hires, illustrating their backgrounds.

However, in the infancy of Amazon, Jeff was looking for excellence without the benefit of the stellar reputation he was to later earn. He needed a complete leap of faith from some deeply talented individuals — Jeff had been researching for talent while he was still in New York. Proactively, he had been seeking the very best. He thought he had found a significantly capable computer techie in Shel Kaphan. Jeff hoped he would be able to help develop the technical architecture of their new organization. Jeff sat down with Santa Cruz resident over a breakfast of blueberry pancakes. This was a social, charming beginning to the internment of the man many consider to be a co-founder of Amazon in all but name. Jeff's charisma paid off. He convinced the talented, soft-spoken Shel Kaphan to uproot from his California home and join his venture in Seattle. Jeff once called Kaphan the most important person in the history of his company Amazon. Shel's work would make the intricate back end systems of Amazon possible while working on top of the cobweb of extension cords that ran through Jeff's garage.

Kaphan remembers there had just been some vague buzz in the economic community about this new thing called the "web," and people wanted to get in on it. Shel recounts that no one had any idea how big Amazon was going to get or how successful it would be. His co-workers at Apple IBM in California thought he was crazy to join the venture. He can remember the spreadsheets that Jeff used in his attempts to recruit him; he notes that not even Jeff's vision encompassed what they would achieve.

Eventually, the potbellied stove was replaced by a series of space heaters placed throughout the garage of their rented home. The heaters only added to the crisscrossing network of extension cords and door-desks. Jeff's wife Mackenzie remembered that they were running so much power out of the garage that she couldn't use her hair dryer or vacuum their home without blowing a fuse out.

When Shel first arrived, they didn't even have computers in the garage yet. They went shopping. They had to decide what database would be most helpful and figure out how to build a website. Amazingly, at this time it wasn't even largely known how to begin to build a website. Shel set about to learn the necessary code. The initial employees really were working from scratch as they developed the tech to sell books online. For his second hire, Jeff looked to an employee with the

University of Washington, Paul Davis. The venture was so risky for Paul that when he was leaving his job, his co-workers thought he was crazy for joining Jeff. The university employees passed around a coffee can to collect money. They said that it would be something for Paul to fall back on in case the bottom fell out of the startup. Paul was also an investment in the company's back end development. He was quintessential in getting the fledgling online book store off the ground and turned into a reality.

The coding, the business planning, and work were consuming, but Jeff never lost perspective. Shel remembers one morning he came in and Jeff said that today they wouldn't be working on coding. Instead, he planned for them to hike Mt. Rainier. They drove the three hours out to the mountain's base summit at Paradise Inn and did a day hike, just enjoying the fabulously beautiful scenery of Washington.

Although financially successful from the beginning, being part of Amazon's startup was not glamorous. Mackenzie remembers the founding stages all too well. Mackenzie says she remembers, "when he (Jeff) wrote the business plan, and I worked with him and many others represented in the converted garage." Mackenzie recalls them operating out of, "the basement warehouse closet, the barbecue-scented offices, the Christmas-rush distribution centers, and the door-desk filled conference rooms in the early years..." Mackenzie performed the company's initial accounting and bookkeeping— they were keeping it in the family at the outset of Amazon's venture.

The new team developed and experimented with their creation of an online book store. When they felt confident that they had achieved what they were looking for, Jeff felt ready for testing. They recruited three hundred people for beta testing the new web site. Once more, Jeff reached out to his friends and family for help in testing the new Amazon structure; the users found that it worked seamlessly. The coders had been successful in their venture. They had created a user-friendly experience that had achieved the level of customer service ready tech that Jeff had imagined from the very beginning.

On July 5, 1995, the day after Independence Day and a little less than a year after his fateful road trip, Jeff founded Amazon with absolutely no press. Amazon boasted a million titles. This was an impressive thirty percent of the full three million titles that were available worldwide. Jeff's dream of creating an online book store that featured more titles than could possibly exist in a physical book store had finally come true. In the enterprising spirit of a startup, the few employees were physically packaging and driving books to the post office to be mailed. Jeff remembered that in the infantile stages of planning, one of Jeff's New York colleagues had ordered a book online. It had arrived a full two weeks later — and the thing was badly damaged in the shipping process. The new Amazon model was going to fill a badly needed hole in the book production field. However, they had to survive as a startup first.

Despite the fact that the website was launched without any fanfare, the Amazon website flourished. They succeeded to conquer the online book market through word of mouth and person-to-person email chains. The total lack of local public attention didn't hurt the site, and it garnered instant business. Jeff remembers, in the beginning, that they were excited to have sold a book as far as New Hampshire. Initially, Jeff had rigged a bell to sound whenever they made a sale. However, they were so successful that the constant ringing of the bell became an annoyance and they quickly disabled it. Within thirty days, the company had sold to all fifty states and forty-five countries. They were quickly doing twenty thousand dollars of business a week. Jeff remembers knowing at that point that they had something special, that they had developed a niche market that would exceed their wildest hopes.

The startup required an almost relentless pace to succeed.

Employees worked sixty plus hours, often opting to just sleep inside of their cars before returning to work the next day. Friends and family pitched in to make the holiday rush possible, while steady employees rotated the graveyard shift to make sure shipping demands were met. Jeff felt significantly burned out by this initial holiday pressure and continues to this day to hire vast amounts of workers to prevent putting so much demand on Amazon employees ever again.

Keeping an eye toward frugality, but recognizing the need to expand their space from his home, Jeff moved the offices downtown. Amazon could now boast ten employees, and they needed space to keep up with demand. However, their first location out of Jeff's garage was in a deeply shady area— the new company's headquarters had upgraded in terms of space, but they were in a neighborhood with a heroin needle exchange.

The very success that Jeff had achieved proved to be an obstacle. He began to achieve the notice of the bookselling community, where he was quickly gaining ground. It didn't take long for the fledgling organization to face backlash from those they were competing with. Jeff was struggling in an economic pool that was dominated by titanic booksellers that had risen a few short years before. These colossal book venues had themselves transformed bookselling in a short-lived wave, creating mass-scale book stores and putting small booksellers out of the market. They were not interested in brooking any competition in the field from online sales. Their monumental sales threatened the very existence of brick-and-mortar book sale monoliths. Jeff remembers that they were threatened with lawsuits from Barnes and Noble and Borders books. Resentment from competitors prompted Jeff to defend Amazon's expansion. He quipped that "Amazon isn't happening to the book business," Jeff believes it is the "The future (that) is happening to the book business." But the newly crowned book barons felt threatened just the same. Jeff invited the notorious Riggio brothers of Barnes and Noble books to dinner in Seattle. They hoped to reach some sort of amicable agreement. The toughened brothers hailed from the New York Bronx; they were famous for their polished suits and ruthless business tactics. The new Amazon employees decided on a tactful and flattering approach to the dinner. The brothers told Jeff that they were going to obliterate Amazon, but the meeting went well enough that there was an initial discussion of an online partnership. However, following an email exchange, this fell through. As evidence of the Riggio's competitive spirit: when Barnes and Noble did finally build a website the Riggio brothers floated calling their website— predator books. It is ironic to note that most of Jeff's early meetings occurred at the Barnes and Noble Starbucks.

Outsiders began to speculate that Amazon's decline was only a matter of time. They nicknamed Amazon's website, Amazon.toast. The common belief was that once Barnes and Noble and Borders entered the online game, Amazon would be a passing economic star, quickly to be forgotten. However, Jeff believed that through remaining innovative he would be able to stay ahead of the established booksellers. Jeff would one day be quoted as saying that they work to focus on the customer, while the competition was distracted by Amazon's success—In 1996 Amazon had made 15.7 million dollars in sales and had one hundred employees.

Later that year, in 1997, Amazon went national; it opened its second distribution center in New Castle, Delaware. Ever financially cautious, Jeff chose a state where his customers wouldn't have to pay sales tax on the items that they purchased. Delaware had the added advantage of serving the East Coast easily, and customers would quickly receive their orders. Although Delaware was meant to be an East Coast facet, the 200,000 square foot facility would touch nearly every state in the union with its sales. In fact, Jeff's emphasis on customer satisfaction drove delivery speeds to legendary heights. Customers would marvel over the arrival of packages that they hadn't expected for days.

However, the new company faced power outages, and employees would let packages sit around warehouses for hours at a time. Eerily as Jeff introduced kitchen items to the Amazon venture, knives would sometime come hurtling down conveyor belts.

With every year, Jeff brought more significant changes to the face of Amazon. In 1998, he introduced the CD's and DVD's that his new tagline advertised. The new music/film element of the store carried one hundred and twenty-five thousand titles. Jeff's ambition to create a book store that couldn't exist in physical space had been rendered in the music and movie industry. His selection bypassed any other physical music store out there. With his ear toward customer preferences, Jeff created an option for customers to listen to song clips before their purchase and to choose music based on their mood.

In what would become another momentous decision, Jeff polled buyers about things that they wanted Amazon to begin selling. He received a series of unconnected, un-patterned requests for purchases. In particular, Jeff remembers one customer asking the online book store if they would carry windshield wipers — he was looking for an online place to purchase them for his car.

Jeff, instead of laughing off the eclectic cornucopia of requests, saw an opportunity. He knew that customers were looking to the internet market place for convenient purchasing on an expanse of items. He wanted to fill the niche. The continuation of the concept of what Jeff would call his "Everything Store," was born. Eventually, the company's logo would be a yellow arrow that looks like a smile underneath the Amazon letters. Originally, the smile design meant that "we're happy to deliver anything, anywhere." However, an Amazon release expanded the meaning by emphasizing that the beginning of the smile/arrow started at the "A" and ended at the "Z "of "Amazon." This was meant to indicate that Amazon had everything to fulfill its customers' needs from A through Z. During the year 1999, Jeff expanded the store to include toys and electronics. They had grown to employ over 3,000 workers— some of whom were operating out of the United Kingdom and Germany. Amazon had an astounding year, they reached six hundred and ten million dollars in sales. That same year, Jeff secured a significant patent: his one mouse click online check out. Called the 1-click, Jeff successfully carried suits against companies that adopted his site's checkout method. Specifically, Jeff was successful in suing Barne's and Noble for using his tech innovation. The company was forced to lease Amazon's patent until the patent expired eighteen years later.

In a 1999 article that year, Jeff told media source *Entrepreneur*," We are trying to innovate in the e-commerce arena. That's our heritage— We are building something that can't be pigeonholed—We defy easy analogy. It's not a vision that can be communicated in a sound bite; we want to be the most customer-centric company in the world: Come and discover and buy anything online."

Later in 1999, Jeff instituted yet another company innovation in the form of his third-party market places: outside individuals could hawk their eclectic wares using the framework of the Amazon workplace. It was a dynamite financial decision. In the first four months of its infancy, a quarter of a million people utilized what would come to be known as the Marketplace to purchase items from Amazon. Jeff innovated web purchasing with his customer-centric attitude. He introduced web purchasing innovations that were to become standardized parts of the e-commerce experience. He invented online customer reviews, recommended books to buyers based on their previous selections, and had customers receive email confirmations after sales. His innovations paid off. He was achieving wild financial success that year, but things took a dark turn in December.

In the midst of his success, Jeff was facing yet another crisis.

After a historic year of market innovation, the Dotcom bubble was about to burst. All of his success was feared to be hollow. Amazon had yet to turn a profit as a company. The Dotcom bust was directly overlapping the rise of Amazon. Other fledgling businesses were trying their hands at e-commerce. Giddy investors threw money at these dawning internet businesses, placing far too much confidence and too many investments in untested ventures. These startups also made glaring early errors. One memorable company made the mistake of immediately trying to operate out of eighteen countries. One infamous Dotcom that went up in flames was founder Kaleil Tuzman's govWorks. He burned through sixty million dollars in venture capital… and never turned a dime back to his investors. Tuzman's fall has been truly meteoric. His rise in the Dotcom world ended catastrophically; he now faces twenty years of jail time. This, after being extradited from a Columbian jail, where he had fled and was hiding out— He was sharing a cell with a convicted murderer when his extradition came through. These economic fires burned and defined investments for a generation.

Many of these companies had firework-like-success only to go up in flames in a matter of years. In characteristic caprice, the market decided that these new tech companies weren't worth what had initially been projected— This spooked investors and the Dotcom bubble burst, leaving behind a terrific wake in the e-commerce world. Doubtless, Jeff faced the issue of reassuring his own investors that Amazon was not one of these shooting star ventures. Especially, this task would have been daunting considering that despite sales, he had yet to turn a profit.

However, later that same month, December 1999, Jeff received the crowning achievement to his professional success: excitingly, Jeff was named *Time* magazine's "Person of the Year" for his innovation in the e-commerce market and transformation of the book sales industry. They called him, "the king of cyber commerce," and at the age of 35, Jeff was the fourth youngest person ever to receive that award.

The following year, Jeff's childhood lifelong dream of entering the space race was initiated with the founding of his endeavor: Blue Origin. Only thirty years after first viewing the newscast of Neil Armstrong taking his first steps on the moon, Jeff's passions had won out. He had officially entered the space race. The organization was set up to make commercial space flights an affordable venture for the public, with the ultimate goal of boosting the practicality of space colonization.

Jeff was earning the title of King of Commerce. He was rapidly expanding Amazon to include items such as clothing, and he was eager to adapt and adopt further. However, he still had a big problem. Although the new company was making mind-blowing sales and almost single-handedly pioneering the e-commerce platform, they had yet to operate in the black.

Naysayers began to predict that instead of Amazon.toast they could start calling it Amazon.bomb. They believed Jeff's work was going to go the way the rest of the internet bubble had gone. And their dark speculations seemed confirmed when in the early 2000s Jeff tightened Amazon's belt, laying off a number of employees. Eventually, Amazon would have to lay off an investor alarming fifteen percent of employees. During the bust, Amazon's share dropped a stomach-clenching fall from one hundred and seven dollars a share to just seven dollars a share. The company lost $1.4 billion dollars that year. This was one of the wildest bends that Amazon would face in it's meteoric success story.

The experiment in 2000 didn't just look like failure, it looked like it had caused an explosion and then set fire to a lot of financial lives. However, Jeff asserted: "In business, you need to be able to go forward without looking back. Everyone has regrets; there's no doubt that this will happen." He says that. "In order to be successful an individual needs to be able to press forward and not allow those thoughts to otherwise taint the opportunities that can help them to achieve their goals—

Looking back is something you can do when you've reached your goal or are otherwise done moving forward — if such a day comes. Until then, regrets cannot be a part of the equation."

However, despite the hardship, Jeff remained committed to the basic principles of success that he had started with. He especially highlighted the importance of maintaining his customer service commitment. Once more his foresight and business acumen worked. And despite the shattering of the Dotcom bust, amazingly, Jeff's Amazon turned its first profit just a year later in 2001. Once Amazon turned this curve, and they had become profitable, Jeff's success seemed like it could reach no limit. Jeff had built his empire in just five years. The billion plus loss of just the year before was quickly forgotten in what would be a dizzying accumulation of wealth and economic progress.

This rapid empire conquest caused Jeff and his employees to live at glaringly high-stress levels. Humorously, one manager recounts that part of the stress relief for employees was that he encouraged primal screams. He even allowed anyone that had achieved something significant to call him and scream into the phone; he has noted that some of the screaming almost shattered his speakers.

Amazon continued to explode: Jeff added clothes in 2002. He

partnered with major labels like The Gap and Nordstrom to offer a wide range of clothing. In all, he started his new clothing launch offering with 400 clothing labels for his online market place. Amazon began offering jewelry to consumers that year. He had created a full-scale mall experience for customers to shop from the comfort of their homes.

Jeff further expanded this experience; in 2003 he made sporting goods available to the public. It was also in 2003 that Jeff instituted web hosting. He licensed Amazon's platform to other businesses seeking to join the e-commerce trade. Amazon even sold to the book store Border's— Jeff was officially hosting and selling to his former competitors. To this day, Jeff's endeavor with hosting has made Amazon dominant among web hosting services. This source of revenue serves as one of their primary market returns.

In 2004 Jeff took Asia— he purchased Joyo and turned it into Amazon China, attempting to corner the market against giants like Alibaba. The following year in 2005, Jeff made another titanic market decision in the form of Amazon Prime. Amazon Prime instituted a loyalty program that incentivized customers with excellent shipping benefits— For a seventy-nine-dollar annual membership, Prime Members could have free shipping and receive their items within two days. This speed and efficiency was an incredible jump from the startups' initial efforts — where employees (including Jeff) had been hand delivering sales to the post office. Prime, like so many of Jeff's other Amazon endeavors, had meteoric growth — today, it enjoys a global membership of over a hundred million users.

His vision of the "Everything Store" was being fulfilled. However, his greatest impact on the world of books, information access, and e-commerce was still ahead of him. The Kindle. Jeff had had already revolutionized the book buying industry. The launch of the Kindle changed the very way people thought about reading. The term e-books entered the daily vocabulary of readers across the world. Later, Jeff would sign a deal with Wylie publishers that rocked book prices — he angered publishers that felt they weren't getting their fair cut — but readers and authors made gains through this move.

Shortly before Christmas in 2007, Amazon announced that it would be consolidating headquarters in Seattle. The city accommodated this economic powerhouse by raising its height limits on taller buildings. The new complex would host a mini-city of forty thousand employees. The eight million square foot building was a staggering jump from Jeff's poorly insulated garage and its accompanying space heaters. This economic jump is especially impressive considering it hallmarked only twelve years after Jeff started his Amazon venture.

This year, competitor, Borders finally toppled. They declared bankruptcy, making Jeff the almost unquestioned king of book sales. Barnes and Noble continued to stay afloat, but only through mimicking Jeff's strategies. It was widely circulated that they were only afloat through sales of their e-reader, Nook, which was their answer to Jeff's Kindle. The flagging and mirroring of his tactics by competitors had validated Jeff's theory that customer service is more important than a focus on what the competitor is doing.

In 2008, Amazon acquired Audible for about three hundred million dollars, which features audio books and would advance users experience with the Kindle. This innovative inclusion of over eighty thousand titles available in America and Europe was introduced only a couple of months following the release of Jeff's Kindle. Today, Audible maintains an impressive forty-one percent market share of audiobooks.

Jeff found in 2009 that there were still e-commerce lands to conquer: He had not been able to secure the shoe industry. He had been competing with the site Zappos.com for the shoe market, but without successfully subduing it. Zappos had an impressive policy of free returns, and customers could get overnight shipping on shoes. Ultimately, Jeff made the decision to purchase the company outright for nine hundred million dollars— ensuring that Amazon had a dominant place in that industry.

Unsatisfied to simply rest on his laurels with Kindle, in 2010, Jeff introduced the world to the Kindle Fire. The new Kindle fire featured color and LCD lighting. They also evolved into multi-platform tools— movies, music, videos. The personalization of Kindle experienced the same evolution that Jeff's Amazon business had enjoyed.

Apple's CEO Steve Jobs gave Jeff a run for his money with their introduction of the iPad— which housed e-books, but they faced some legal battles as they tried to compete in the e-book industry. However, despite the competition, Amazon's e-book sales reached a staggering 2.38 billion dollars. Thanks to his work, e-books were growing by two hundred percent a year, and Jeff had captured ninety-five percent of the e-book market.

In 2010, Jeff took Amazon into the realm of television production with his instigation of Amazon Productions. Unsatisfied to allow powerhouses like Netflix govern the takeover from cables giants, he looked to crowdsource the making of original tv and feature film content. Amazon's first original feature film was produced and released by the company, in 2015, was Spike Lee's *Chi-Raq*.

In the Spring of 2012, Jeff moved to have Amazon purchase Kiva Systems, a robotics division that he acquired for seven hundred and seventy-five million dollars. The new acquisition allowed Amazon to further streamline its production and reduced the need for human workers. After the acquisition, Jeff severed his partnerships with The Gap and Office Depot. In a characteristically competitive move, he was cornering the market on his newly acquired tech. This dissolution with these partners permitted Amazon to retain the corner on cutting edge delivery tech.

Amazon had a setback in 2012 when they lost funds — investors took a hit over this temporary struggle. However, Jeff's vision that a company is about the long term has resonated with both his investors and his stockholders. By in large, even with this loss, Wall Street did not bat an eye over the downturn. Jeff had earned the confidence of the market.

In a move that surprised some finance watchers, Jeff purchased the Washington Post in 2013. He acknowledged that it wasn't like he usually went around acquiring businesses that were the equivalent of an underwater potato chip stand, but he believed in the free press. He wanted to promote the core values of the Washington Post's work. Later that same year, Jeff began package delivery on Sundays. He eventually took this nationwide, in partnership with USPS.

In August of that year, Amazon's purchase of the video game platform Twitch became a highly successful venture, even at its price tag of nine hundred and seventy million dollars. The platform dovetailed well with Amazon's already successful video gaming division and hosting outlets. It also presented the opportunity to entice the global video gaming community toward Amazon's cloud-based operations.

Once more capitalizing on the holiday season, Jeff introduced his new smart speaker the Echo to the market in 2015. The company was celebrating its twentieth anniversary. Amazon was now worth two hundred and forty-five billion dollars. The Echo market innovation became available in three thousand stores; it served as the tech platform for Amazon's launch of Alexa. Alexa tech was Amazon's personal assistant answer to Siri. Alexa is a convenience for customers, but she works as a data harvesting mechanism for Amazon. Naturally, the customer-oriented Jeff Bezos would capitalize on a platform that would give Amazon greater insights into the habits and needs of his customer base.

Jeff's ambition to achieve the "Everything Store" was being accomplished — He moved into groceries when in 2017 he purchased Whole Foods. With the purchase, Jeff acquired four hundred stores. He had built an empire on excellent customer service and adaptability and told consumers he wanted to implement the same policies at Whole Foods.

Jeff went from an online bookseller to owning a company that boasts over twenty million different items in stock. In testament of the reach of Amazon's expansive selection, humorous online lists of the variety of things available on Amazon began to surface. For example, Amazon followers note that you can purchase, fifteen hundred live ladybugs, a bacon-scented mustache, a yodeling pickle, and a pail of ten preserved crayfish. One list notes that you can purchase both a human bone (for the price of one Kindle book) or curiously uranium, (which costs the same as a suit for blow drying your dog.) One lady operating out of Japan offered a book on crafts to make use of the cat hair your pet she. She enumerated that one can make coasters, finger puppets, tote bags, and picture frames. Her description does humorously note that although she doesn't personally own any cats, she is a renowned pet sitter. Clearly, Jeff's hopes of an "Everything Store" had been more than answered.

In 2018 Jeff decided on yet another expansion of Amazon, he moved to set up a second headquarters. He called the company's newest endeavor, HQ2. This decision set off a local government race to become the new site of the next Amazon locale. His former hometown of Miami, Washington D.C., cities across the mid-west all vied with tax incentives to host Amazon. This race enabled Amazon to harvest data it would never have been able to acquire so effortlessly otherwise. As the competition reached a fever pitch, Jeff announced he would be opening up yet another headquarters. Eventually, D.C. and New York were chosen as natural locations for Amazon.

In September of that year, the company enjoyed a brief high of a trillion-dollar worth - only the second company to ever accomplish that level of economic prosperity. Apple had passed that threshold only months before Amazon. Analysts project that Amazon has the capacity to reach a two-trillion-dollar marker, and they believe that astonishing figure isn't that far away.

It was in the fall of October 2018 that Jeff Bezos became the wealthiest man in the world. His personal fortune was one hundred and sixty billion dollars. Shortly after this hallmark, Jeff's wealth escalated to make him the richest man in modern history. To make this figure more comprehensible, one journalist broke down Jeff's wealth in comparison to the average American.

In 2019 the HQ2 run for New York was halted. Although there was significant backing from locals, especially minority groups, pushback from a small cabal of Congressmen who balked at the tax incentives, unfortunately, prevented the New York headquarters from becoming a reality.

Looking toward the future of Amazon—Jeff says of his company: Evolve or die. This economic Darwinism has reverberated across the economy. Initially, in media interviews, Jeff imagined that his work would supplant only businesses that weren't experience oriented. He was mildly offended by the suggestion that Amazon had made book buying impersonal. Rather, Jeff argued that Amazon had actually made book purchasing more personal than the traditional method of driving to a physical book store. He asserted that in a conventional book market you don't have access to other customer reviews, and you certainly don't have book buyers that have been keeping a list of your previous purchases, while making recommendations for other things you might like. Jeff remarked that "I don't know about you, but most of my exchanges with cashiers are not that meaningful."

Jeff summarized the personal attitude that Amazon takes with its customers with, "You know you're not anonymous on our site." Jeff continued, "We're greeting you by name, showing you past purchases— to the degree that you can arrange to have transparency combined with an explanation of what the consumer benefit is."

It made sense to him that people would continue to want to engage with offline market places, where they could enjoy the social elements of shopping. His example was stores like The Gap, that Jeff believed would always have an element of that niche. However, Jeff did not foresee the expanse to which online shopping would shake even these retailers. He was, nevertheless, almost prophetic in his expectation that users would continue to utilize storefronts that incorporated a user experience element or a social engagement factor. For example, corporate powerhouse partners like Starbucks are moving away from the traditional warehouse model. They are utilizing storefronts where customers can do cupping (coffee tasting) and then later order the products shipped directly to their homes. Most recently Tesla car sales announced that it will be closing many of its dealerships in favor of storefronts that are only utilized as test sites. They are campaigning on user experience, telling customers that they are welcome to borrow a Tesla for a test drive. They invite users to engage socially with their product, perhaps taking a weekend trip with a friend.

This direct to consumer, instantaneous cultural phenomenon and evolving source of consumer expectation was envisioned and catalyzed by Jeff's foresight and drive. This new model will force even more box stores and real estate-based markets to shutter. The goods delivery pace race is being driven by the market's ability to save money by not having to keep vast warehouses of goods on hand, while also meeting customer expectations for customization and speed. Jeff put this phenomenal shift in the economic culture baldly, with four words, "strip malls are dead."

Chapter 3 - Jeff Bezos: Little Known Facts

Jeff can do basic veterinary work on cattle — including vaccinations. He can also fix the plumbing in a pinch.

Jeff once hired a spelling bee champ — he likes to stop her in the hallway with quick spelling challenges like "onomatopoeia."

Jeff owns more land than any other person in the United States — including a three hundred-thousand-acre property in Texas. He has tried to recreate his boyhood ranching experiences that he shared with his grandfather, for whom he is named.

Jeff makes 8,961,187 dollars an hour.

Jeff was part of a study featuring gifted children — the observer noted that although the Tolkien reading sixth grader was confident and articulate, he lacked somewhat in leadership skills. Ironically, he made the great fifty leaders of the world list three years running.

Jeff once survived a helicopter crash— he was out viewing a potential property for his space endeavor Blue Origin when they went down— he says that he was thinking, "what a stupid way to die." He no longer rides in helicopters, but he does take his private jet to travel.

Jeff's helicopter crash was his second near-death experience— a few years before he was in Seattle during a harrowing 6.9 magnitude earthquake. Reportedly, in the middle of the earthquake, he was nearly crushed by a tungsten ball weighing 20 pounds; Jeff had to crawl under a table to get out of its way.

Jeff's current home is on the historical register and used to be a museum— for textiles. (So, clothes)

Jeff says that he developed the space age personal assistant, Alexa, based on the talking computer featured in Star Trek.

Jeff's owns several multi-million-dollar properties around the nation. Some of his neighbors include— Barack & Michelle Obama and Ivanka Trump.

Jeff is dedicated to getting enough sleep— he doesn't use an alarm to wake up. And unlike current inventor and tech pioneer Elon Musk, he commits to eight hours of sleep a night.

Jeff's first book sale at Amazon was about computers: *Fluid Concepts and Analogies*— Computer Models of the Fundamental Mechanisms of Thought

Jeff's fastest order to date: An Amazon customer received a four-pack of Starbucks Vanilla Frappuccino in Miami, Florida— The impressive delivery was made in under 10 minutes.

Amazon's property in Phoenix, Arizona, is 1.2 million square feet, which makes it the equivalent of 28 football fields.

Jeff once hired mobile billboards (billboards on trucks) to drive by Barnes & Noble stores that said: "Can't find that book you wanted?" along with Amazon's web address.

Jeff's Amazon employees spend two days every two years working at the customer service desk. This includes Jeff as CEO— His idea is to help all workers understand the Amazon customer service process more fully.

Jeff launched a quizzical program in 2014 called: Pay to Quit. If an Amazon worker hands in their resignation, they'd get $1,000. The idea is to only have Amazon workers that really want to be there, and he actually raised the incentive to quit in 2017 to be $5,000 — Impressively, less than ten percent of the first wave of staffers offered the deal took them up on it.

Amazon Kindle owners spend approximately twelve hundred dollars a year buying media from Amazon.

A whopping ten percent of all Americans have an Amazon Prime account — which runs about thirteen hundred dollars.

Jeff's ambition as a child was to become an astronaut — in an interview, he told a reporter he'd still like the chance if the opportunity presents itself.

Amazon ships thirty-five items per second, but on one cyber Monday they sold more than three hundred items per second. They ship an incredible six hundred and eight million packages a year.

Amazon is the tenth most visited website in the world—shipping to seventy-five countries and serving two hundred and seventy million active users; the site went down for forty-nine minutes, once, which cost the company five point seven million dollars in sales.

Amazon has an army of fifteen thousand robots that help in the speed of the shipping process.

Jeff and fellow billionaire Mark Cuban once both played their own voice talent for a *Simpson's* episode; Jeff was featured in an episode where the character Mr. Burns goes to billionaire camp.

Jeff had a cameo on *Star Trek Beyond* once— he plays an alien whose line was, "speak normally." He went to the San Diego based comic-con event to watch the showing of the film.

Jeff isn't all that fond of music— this disinterest left the door open for Apple's Steve Jobs to corner the digital music world, although Jeff's powerhouse response was the Kindle.

Amazon employs seven and a half percent of all working adults living in Seattle.

Amazon's cardboard consumption could cover the entire United States with just five months of the boxes it uses: If all the cardboard used in all one point six million daily Amazon packages — including their padded envelopes — sent out was laid out flat, it would cover an area equivalent to over twenty six thousand square miles: which is roughly the same size as the State of West Virginia or the entire country of Sri Lanka.

Amazon offers some pretty oddball items, but one particularly strange product is a husband-replacement pillow to cuddle up with. The smoothie is dressed in a blue business casual oxford.

Jeff Bezos spends one point six million dollars per year on personal security guards to protect him and his family. According to actor Chris Pine, Jeff showed up to the *Star Trek Beyond* set with three limos and nine individual guards.

Jeff can be very secretive — not even sharing company plans with employees.

Jeff once won the prestigious Gregg Zehr award for the innovation of the Amazon Kindle.

Jeff has committed Amazon to hiring Latino engineers— a result of his excellent relationship with his Cuban immigrant stepfather, Mike Bezos.

Chapter 4 - The Tactics and Techniques

Think Long Term:

Inventions by year –

    1901 — Vacuum cleaner

    1902 — Air conditioning; automated tea maker

    1903 — Electrocardiogram; first powered flight

    1904 — Radar; tea bags; diodes

    1905 — Plastic; windscreen wipers; silencer for guns

    1906 — Radio broadcasting

    1907 — Electric washing machine

    1908 — Coffee filter; water coolers; paper cups; assembly line production; the model T –

    first affordable motor car

    1910 — Neon lamps

"And that's a part of our world," entered the daily life of American households with the invention of the radio in 1906.

It was to quickly become the herald, the darling of American homes; citizens were amazed, as it brought opera and ballet music to living rooms. For the first time, Americans that had only traveled an average of fifteen miles from their homes were following news of the conflict with Russia. There was an awe and a pleasure in the amenities of the twentieth century, to which this present century may indulge their pride at their inventive advancements. It was an exciting time to be alive. The patent offices of that era became famous for saying that, "everything that could be invented, had been invented." Although the above timeline may somewhat excuse pardonable pride, it is a sharp lesson in thinking long term about the scope of possibility.

Perhaps Jeff Bezos greatest strength and strongest tactic as an entrepreneur is his ability to think long term. Jeff is forever encouraging professionals to think beyond the short term, the immediately fashionable. It is why he was ultimately so very successful at foreseeing that the internet would be a center for e-commerce, and it was the foundation of ideation for his creation of Amazon. In the nineties he was able to see that the hyper-growth of the internet was just the very dawning of its capacity: "Another thing that I would recommend to people is that they always take a long-term point of view. I think this is something about which there's a lot of controversies. A lot of people — and I'm just not one of them — believe that you should live for the now."

Human beings have a tendency to rest in the immediate, to embrace current fashions and endure the stains on their present time. There are very few born pioneers; most young men must be lead West. Jeff both literally and figuratively pioneered a westward expansion in knowledge. However, Jeff once reflected on this present internet age, comparing it to the self-satisfaction of the previous century.

Despite his accomplishments, Jeff looks forward to the next century with clear-eyed hope for its inventive extension. His long-range view spans both the last century, this present era, and anticipates what's coming. The last century ushered in the advancement of the washing machine, which was brilliant, but limited — users would catch their hair in it, and people would crush their fingers in the gears while rolling their clothes through. Jeff tells us that we are living in a comparative stop gap of internet progress: "But there's so much kludge, so much terrible stuff: we are at the 1908 Hurley washing machine stage with the Internet; that's where we are. We don't get our hair caught in it — but that's the level of primitiveness of where we are. We're in 1908."

Thinking long term means denying the craze around instant gratification: Jeff says that for ultimate satisfaction and success that, "I think what you do is think about the great expanse of time ahead of you and try to make sure that you're planning for that in a way that's going to leave you ultimately satisfied," Jeff continues that, "This is the way it works for me. There are a lot of paths to satisfaction, and you need to find one that works for you."

Amazon definitely had its moments in which investors could have felt justified in doubting the range of Jeff's vision. Despite the accolades that Jeff was receiving throughout the nineties it took a number of years, millions of dollars in loss, and incremental failures for the company to gain the momentum Jeff had foreseen. But he never wavered: "To be profitable (now) would be a bad decision," Jeff said in an almost cheeky interview. "This is a critical formative time if you believe in investing in the future," Jeff commented to one media outlet— that it is a challenge to get investors, individuals to share your scope of the future and be content to wait for financial and inventive success.

Foresight isn't enough— Jeff says that it also takes terrific commitment to the details for success to be achieved: Amazon's invention of the Kindle, for instance, is a product of Jeff internalizing hundreds of data points; he understood from his analyses that millions of people would want an electronic book reader that could download any work in an impressive sixty seconds or less. Jeff aimed for that delivery target without ever feeling impeded by the technical issues like the right compression ratios or transmission speeds for the Kindle's book files. His engineers were given free rein to solve technical challenges as they thought best. Jeff just asked that they develop their work to make it right for the customer. The long term, arduous commitment to getting the Kindle right took years, while Amazon was mastering the hardware necessary to build these electronic advancements, but Jeff never blinked. In the face of doubt, Jeff was once asked by one finance executive how much he was willing to spend on the project, and Jeff fired back at him: "How much do we have?"

Jeff notes that there will always be resistance to business plans that take a long-term approach. It goes very much against the grain in most investors. He once laughed that, "Get rich slowly schemes are not big sellers on infomercials." He cautions professionals that whatever the speed of Amazon's inventiveness may look like — all of his overnight success moments are the product of ten years of work and investment.

Self-Improvement:

Perhaps the greatest maker of a successful and worthwhile human being is the humility to see the need to change and to commit to do better in the future. Jeff Bezos does not exempt his personal faults from the need to listen to criticisms and adapt. Sometimes this humility has extended itself in humorous adaptations like in Jeff's pursuit of women, sometimes this has been very serious — like his commitment to be a gentler communicator, and at other times the adaptations have been downright fun — like the transformation of Jeff's physical appearance.

One comical example of Jeff's commitment to self-improvement was his proactive approach to dating — developing his "women flow" method. In true Jeff Bezos fashion, he analytically decided at 27 years old that it was time that he got married. What does a business-minded; space tech-loving man want in a wife? He asked his friends to set him up on dates with women that could get him out of a third world prison. He says that "Life is too short to hang out with people that aren't resourceful." In other words, he wanted to marry someone that was highly inventive. His work on Wall Street led him to facetiously develop the "women flow," method — playing on investor's methods of choosing and making good financial bets. Proactive as ever, Jeff took ballroom dancing lessons to improve his stock.

Jeff laughed that so very many blind dates followed after this. He said he got really good at them: Jeff said that he got so good at the blind dates game that he ended up only dating people that were also just really terrific at doing blind dates. They would phase each other out as future partners within eight minutes. Self-deprecatingly, Jeff remembered that: "I'm a very goofy sort of person in many ways; I tell duff jokes. I kind of have to grow on somebody — I'm not the kind of person you meet and kind of go, 'Oh I love this guy!' and it's great, and you go home and tell all your girlfriends about him. That's not me."

The "women flow" method was ultimately unsuccessful, but it's indicative of Jeff's commitment to self-improve. He tells leaders today that an important tactic is to face personal flaws even when it's embarrassing or difficult: He says that "leaders listen attentively, speak candidly, and treat others respectfully— They are vocally self-critical, even when doing so is awkward or embarrassing; leaders do not believe their or their team's body odor smells of perfume; they benchmark themselves and their teams against the best." The remark that Amazon doesn't treat body odor like its perfume is a very direct way of telling managers at the company that when something smells, it's counterproductive to pretend otherwise.

Jeff challenged himself to address his own flaws in what was probably less charming than the process of learning ballroom dancing - improving his leadership style. For illustration, India in the 1630s was famous for its juggernauts. In parades, worshippers of Krishna pulled a behemoth depiction of the god on wheels through the streets. They would sometimes be crushed by it during the procession. The deaths of the worshippers have become a modern metaphor for institutions that sacrifice followers in the name of progress.

Comparatively, it would be simple for Jeff to live as a corporate juggernaut. He is absolutely a driven, successful human being, and with that drive and determination, it would be easy to excuse steamrolling and treating others harshly.

And Jeff has definitely had his harsh moments. At Amazon, he will go on rants when employees underperform. Internally these are called "nutters." This aspect of his leadership style has been something that he struggled with in the past. Business Insider once compiled a list of his most direct, hard moments:

— Are you lazy or just incompetent?
— Do I need to go down and get the certificate that says I'm CEO of the company to get you to stop challenging me on this?
— (After reviewing the annual plan from the supply chain team) I guess supply chain isn't doing anything interesting next year.
— (After reading a start-of-meeting memo, he remarked that) This document was clearly written by the B team. Can someone get me the A team document? I don't want to waste my time with the B team document.
— (Following an engineer's presentation) Why are you wasting my life?

One of Jeff's flaws as a leader is his overly direct, sometimes harsh approach to failure in his subordinates, but Jeff listened to these critiques on his personality… even when that was an embarrassing or awkward process. He hired a leadership coach to help him improve his style. Jeff knows that he doesn't want to lead in a way that rolls over other people in the procession of progress.

Another interesting aspect of Jeff's commitment to self-improvement is his physical appearance. Although he initially represented a quintessential techie programmer: pale, thin, and with a somewhat wasted physique, Jeff has transformed himself. He has worked out, with one journalist describing him as ripped enough to star in the *Fast and the Furious* film series.

Life Long Reader:

Jeff is a lifelong learner and lover of books, which contributed to his ability to think critically and long term. He was a lover of the classics as a child— Tolkien's, *Hobbit* and all things space formed his young mind. Jeff said that "You know, we love stories and we love narrative; we love to get lost in an author's world." Later, he founded a startup Summer Camp as a boy, that emphasized classical literature. He had the fifth and sixth graders read works like The Lord of the Rings novel by J. R. R. Tolkien, Stranger in a Strange Land, by Robert A. Heinlein, along with other classic writers like Dickens, Swift, T. H. White, Richard Adams, and Robert Louis Stevenson. He told parents these classics serve as a foundation for critical thinking.

Jeff says that he is a methodical individual, and the methods he adopts are borrowed from books. Despite Jeff's incredible level of productivity as Amazon's CEO, the head of the world's largest bookstore still finds time to read. Jeff buys about 10 books a month — although he usually reads only three. He continues to recommend that individuals learn through literature and use it as a decision-making knowledge base.

As a powerhouse CEO he recommends to fellow readers:
- *The Remains of the Day*, by Kazuo Ishiguro
- *Dune*, by Frank Herbert
- *Built to Last: Successful Habits of Visionary Companies*, by James C. Collins and Jerry I. Porras.

In further evidence of his passion for books: literature loving Jeff, grew up to marry an authoress Mackenzie, and to found Amazon from Seattle, one of the world's most literate, book-hungry cultures — and to revolutionize book buying. It is no wonder that one of Jeff's greatest advancements was book-centered: The Kindle and Kindle Fire are testaments to a literature minded individual. He has been described as altering the very definition of books, but he says that "I think the definition of a book is changing. But I'm skeptical that the novel will be 're-invented."

From book, Jeff says he has drawn two key lessons:
  — To learn and to be curious is one of Jeff's leadership mantras to Amazon management to this day.
  — The ability to think critically

Be Kind:

One of the charming, formative elements of Jeff's childhood was his grandparent's membership in an Airstream club. Hundreds of airstreams looking like a vast centipede, chugging along old U.S. highway routes. On one road trip, Jeff remembers that he turned to his grandmother to tell her that he had made a calculation. He told her he could predict how many years she would lose off her life based on the number of cigarettes that she had smoked.

Jeff remembers that he had expected his grandparents to be impressed with his math skills, but later his grandfather sat him down for a private talk. He told the boy that he was going to be tempted to be seduced by his gifts. But he encouraged Jeff not to let his abilities sway him from being a decent human being. His grandfather told Jeff, you are going to find that, "it is harder to be kind than to be cruel."

This advice — to value and strive for kindness — is something Jeff has tried to live by. He would later pass along the expression that it is harder to be kind than to be cruel at one graduation commencement. Kindness has defined his customer service model with Amazon, and it has become an emblem of the way that he treats individuals in his personal life.

Jeff also passes on his grandfather's advice to his four children. He tells them that it isn't their abilities that define them — it's their choices. Kindness rather than skill is how they should define their worth.

Be Humble:

It was Kim "Dotcom" Schmitz's thirty-fifth birthday. He was one of the Dotcom era's multi-million dollar success stories. He had a spring water-filled pool, a car garage that had a glass-tiled floor that contained 18 luxury cars, one room had seven sixty inch televisions, he had secret passages, he once bought NZ$500,000 of fireworks which he watched from his private helicopter. He had the largest television in New Zealand at the foot of his bed and massive giraffe statues in his mansion gardens. These were just some of the lavish furnishings of his country estate. But on his birthday, police found Kim in his safe room with a loaded gun, waiting for their arrival. Kim was reaping the whirlwind after his binge on investors' money to an amount of roughly $137 million dollars. He was eventually sentenced to prison for insider trading.

Jeff Bezos at thirty-five years old was a very different picture. One journalist remembers that he sat, "in a poorly lit office behind a light-colored desk constructed from a door propped up by two-by-fours. The office is cluttered with stacks of papers and books; the carpet is stained and littered. A yellow rubber duck sits atop a massive gray computer monitor. To his right, hanging lopsided on the wall is a white sign with "amazon.com" spray-painted in blue."

This clearly wasn't the tailored image of a CEO experiencing conspicuous consumption. It wasn't an aesthetically promising picture, but Jeff's humble approach toward company spending has paid off, and modesty has helped make Jeff what he is today. Poetically, this highly memorable, harsh news caster's description usually makes the rounds of the internet when Jeff has made another astonishing milestone in his fabulous career with Amazon.

Specifically, Jeff's modest approach was detailed in a 2012 interview with Forbes. Jeff reported that his salary was only $81,840 and that he hadn't had a raise since 1998. Throughout his historically unparalleled meteoric rise, Jeff stayed very grounded. He became famous for being driven into work by his wife, Mackenzie. She drove Jeff into his Amazon offices in their beat up 1996 Honda, and then she dropped their four children off at school. Mackenzie kept this up until 2013.

Early into the rapid rise of Amazon, Jeff was asked what it was like to have gained such fabulous wealth? He replied that not much has changed, except that he no longer looks at the price of food on the menu. It takes a lot of humility to be a lifelong learner, but humility also gives individuals the freedom from fear to try hard things. Jeff demonstrates that humility is the key to leadership— it frees one to try things that might fail. Jeff says that "People who are right most of the time are people who change their minds often." Jeff asserts that it takes courage to admit when you are wrong and adapt. This common sense, humble approach to business was an impressively far cry from the Dotcom captains' extravagant lifestyles, and it has served Jeff well.

Think Around Problems:

Jeff's mother was always challenged as to ways to stay a step ahead of, or at least next to, her gifted son. He was forever tinkering, as a child inventor. "I think single-handedly we kept many Radio Shacks in business," she joked. At one-point, Jeff became obsessed with a toy called the Infinity Cube, which used motorized mirrors to allow the user to stare out into "infinity." But for the family, the twenty-dollar price tag was too steep. Undaunted, Jeff figured out that the pieces of the cube could be bought cheaply — which he did — and then proceeded to build the cube himself. As a boy Jeff commented that," The way the world is, you know, someone could tell you to press the Button," he said at the time. "You have to be able to think ... for yourself."

This Infinity Cube is emblematic if Jeff's ability to find a way out to achieve your ambitions. With Amazon, he made connecting the pieces of the economy to customer's needs into an art form. He would later tell employees that often the way to get out of a box is to invent your way out.

Hire Well:

"It would be impossible to produce results in an environment as dynamic as the Internet without extraordinary people," Bezos wrote of Amazon's workforce, which in three years had ballooned to 2,100 people — "Setting the bar high in our approach to hiring has been, and will continue to be, the single most important element of Amazon.com's success."

Jeff has been using the Socratic method during the hiring

process since the very beginning, using interview questions that elicit a learning process for the interviewer and the candidate. From its inception Jeff has utilized three key questions in determining whom to hire:

A. Will you admire this person?
B. Will this person raise the average level of effectiveness of the group they're entering?
C. Along what dimension might this person be a superstar?

Another popular interview tactic that Jeff employs is asking candidates to create an action plan as brand managers in a field where they lack any direct knowledge — and then being told they have zero budget to create their product. This method culls those that can't work in an ambiguous environment or fail to be able to innovate.

More than twenty years after he developed this model, Jeff still says that: "Setting the bar high in our approach to hiring has been and will continue to be, the single most important element of Amazon.com's success." And Jeff was correct. His steady, high standards for finding deeply talented individuals has been elemental in his success story.

More specifically, Jeff explains that one of Amazon's core leadership principles is to hire and develop the best — He summarizes what he wants from hiring managers and company leaders with, "Leaders raise the performance bar with every hire and promotion...," He continues, that, "They recognize exceptional talent, and willingly move them throughout the organization."

Have Very High Standards:

They say to make goals measurable: Jeff has that to a tee — Amazon tracks its performance against an impressive five hundred measurable goals. Nearly eighty percent of these goals relate to their customer objectives. Some Amazon workers aim to reduce out-of-stock merchandise, while others are employed to build a bigger library of downloadable films. Impossibly intricate algorithms turn one group of customers' past habits into specialized, custom recommendations for new shoppers. Hourly bestseller lists tell avid readers what is hot from authors. Amazon's weekly reviews track who is on course for their goals, and where they need to take corrective measures. Jeff's workers are so confident in their ability to personalize the site for each customer that the company hardly ever creates stereotypical profiles of users. In other words, some sites would have profiles like "soccer moms" or "high school band geeks," but such marketing standbys are underspecified for Jeff.

He pays even more attention to prevent the things that customers don't want. Jeff says what they hate is delays, getting products with defects and being told that what they want is out-of-stock. This means that the metrics patrol at Amazon religiously tracks the company's numbers. They are looking to make those issues a scarce thing for consumers. Their work is extremely necessary in terms of profit — even the tiniest delay in loading a web page isn't trivial. Amazon has staff have demonstrated that a 0.1-second delay in a page means a one percent drop in customer activity. In a multi-million-dollar industry that translates to tens of thousands of lost profits.

Jeff says that Amazon's leaders are relentlessly committed to the company's high standards - but he realizes that many people think these bars are unreasonably high. However, Jeff says that seasoned leaders are always seeking to raise the bar and aid their teams to achieve high-quality products, services, and results. Management ensures that defective products do not get sent down the line, and they make sure that issues are fixed so that they stay fixed.

But Jeff says that sustaining a culture of high standards is worth it, and he encourages his managers that there are many benefits. He says that obviously high standards mean the company is going to build better products and services for customers. Jeff says that this should be reason enough! But perhaps a little less obvious, employees are drawn to these high standards. They help Amazon with its recruiting and retention. Still more subtle, according to Jeff, is that a culture of high standards is protective of what he calls — all the "invisible" but deeply crucial work that goes on at Amazon and in every company. He means the work that goes unseen. The work that gets done when no one is there to watch. In this kind of environment, doing work well becomes its own reward - it's part of what it means to be a professional at Amazon.

A high standards culture means that the details are important — one Amazon insider remembers a relentless push for sturdier-than-usual cardboard so customers could reuse its boxes for other shipments or presents. This creates goodwill in the customer, but it also puts Amazon's name in front of a second set of potential customers. For example, a sturdy box can be used to take items to a thrift store, for moving, as packaging for a gift. In each avenue, Amazon's branding is being promoted on the side of box.

Work Ethic:

Jeff once summed up his work with, "Work hard, have fun, make history." Even as a young man on Wall Street as Jeff was transitioning from professional success to professional success, he was earning a reputation as a capable and brilliant worker. One fellow worker remembered Jeff as an independent thinker and a highly analytical problem solver — he said that you could just give him a problem and he would gnaw it like a bone. Jeff was a deeply dedicated worker, he initially kept a sleeping bag in his office, prepared to let the work days roll together whenever necessary. It would later be reported that this sleeping bag was as useful as much as it was a picture of his commitment to the work that he was doing.

Work ethic is part of Jeff's ability to innovate. He combines work ethic with innovation when he encourages Amazon employees to increase experimentation from ten to one thousand. He says the more that the company works to experiment the greater chance that they will have success. One of their most successful experimental endeavors was web hosting. Jeff hosted for companies that ranged from selling web services from NASA to Netflix. For space loving Jeff, processing data for NASA must have been a thrill. In one instance, NASA's Cassini space probes had explored Saturn. They garnered raw data of 180,000 photos, and Amazon's computers processed the data within an impressive five hours. Jeff did the job at the cost of less than two hundred dollars. NASA said that doing the work in house would have taken about two weeks.

Family Support is Key:

One of the initial challenges Jeff faced in founding Amazon was garnering funds for his startup. He initially invested ten thousand dollars of his own money into the new venture, but this was just a portion of what Jeff would need to make Amazon a success. He knew that in asking friends and family to be part of this experiment that there was every concern that this endeavor might not make it. There is a fail rate of startups of fifty percent within four years, and at that time the e-commerce trade had never even been tested. Jeff was abandoning his financial security and was faced with possibly jeopardizing the savings of those closest to him if his business endeavor went south.

Nevertheless, for seed money, Jeff eventually managed to garner one million dollars from friends and family. His parents, Mike and Jackie, were initially skeptical about the venture. They knew he had a great job in New York, and they thought he should stay with it. However, although they were hesitant about Jeff quitting and about this new venture— they always believed that Jeff could succeed. His parents gave him two hundred and forty-five thousand dollars to get started. They put themselves at great risk to support Jeff's ingenuity. They had given him their life savings, which represented their retirement money. Jeff had cautioned each of his investors that there was a seventy percent chance that this new venture was going to fail. He told his parents I want you to know the risk. I don't want to come home some day, and you are angry at me over our Thanksgiving meal. This was a fair fear; the internet was a Wild West at this time. The web was as of yet undeveloped, unregulated, and untested. E-commerce was still in the very beginning of its genesis. His siblings and parents were vested in his success though. Touchingly, Jeff's mother would later remark that they weren't betting on the internet. They were betting on their belief in their son.

Their confidence in their son paid off. It is unknown how much Mike and Jackie Bezos are worth officially today, but if they kept all their initial stock, they are worth about 30 billion dollars. As a result, the Bezos couple has the Bezos Family Foundation that they operate. They use their funds for philanthropic aid to others. Thus far, they have donated sixty-five million dollars to promote cancer research.

Additionally, they are focused on promoting learning by providing significant scholarships to students. They focus on scholastic endeavors ranging from conservation issues like preserving the ocean to neuroscience. As a couple, they are still successfully fostering bright minds. They remain close to their son to this day.

Focus on Your Passions:

Jeff says that, "As with all things you need to have some sense of passion for what you do— In order to really get into what you do and enjoy the process you need to be passionate about what you are doing; without passion, business becomes rote and mechanical: a process that holds little joy other than the money that is earned and the chance to earn more. In other words, it becomes a pointless race to whatever end awaits, a meaningless existence that begins with the sunrise and ends with the sunset each passing day."

He continues that in life, "You can have a job, or you can have a career, or you can have a calling, and the best thing is to have a calling; if you find your passion, you'll have that, and all your work won't feel like work to you." However, Jeff found out during his time at Princeton that passions can shift.

Jeff had followed his hero Stephen Hawking's footsteps to Princeton, where he planned to mirror the great man's degree in physics. However, he remembers that he had been struggling over an algebra problem for three hours. He finally decided to call his Sri Lankan friend Yasantha Rajakarunanayake. Mr. Rajakarunanayake was able to do the problem in seconds. Jeff asked him if he had done all of the algebra in his head? Mr. Rajakarunanayake shook his head and said that would be impossible; he had solved a similar math problem several years before, and he had been able to determine from that experience that the answer was "cosine."

It was a life-changing experience for Jeff. He realized he was never going to be able to work as a theoretical physicist. Humbly, he acknowledged later that there were probably two or three geniuses there in the room with him, but this was not the way that his mind worked. It was in this career turning moment that Jeff found the conviction that someday he would start his own business. Years later, Jeff cheerfully shared this story at a commencement speech. Mr. Rajakarunanayake laughingly reached out to say that it was good that Jeff had the courage to pursue his strengths or Amazon would never have been conceived.

Jeff recounted that "Mediocre theoretical physicists make no progress. They spend all their time understanding other people's progress," but he was not bitter about the realization. He humbly described watching others excel as theoretical physics as watching something graceful and awe-inspiring — It was intriguing to him to watch how other people's brains were wired. Accordingly, he switched to a double major: his love for and history with computers won out. He became a computer science and electrical engineering major. In the early nineties, this was a very confident gamble. Individuals of this era still believed that the internet was a fad. That much of this tech would rise, fall, and then be forgotten.

Chapter 5 - 20 Pieces of Advice for Lasting Success

The wealthiest man in modern history, the founder and CEO of Amazon, Time Magazine's Person of the Year, Harvard's "Best Performing CEO," the inventor of the "Everything Store," and one of the leading pioneers of internet commerce is also highly articulate. He has spelled out for Amazon and future leaders how to achieve success professionally and in today's tech-driven culture. One of Jeff's favorite quotes is that " is eighty IQ points," by which Jeff means that achieving a proper perspective is one of the great keys to achieving real results in life.

Kindly, Jeff is free with offering advice to help shape future leaders' perspectives. His advice is keen, but his work and life speak for themselves. The pointers included here are those that he provides his own leadership team at Amazon and individuals that want to mirror his success. They are pieces of wisdom that he has learned through his own experience, and he has implemented to make Amazon the success that it has become. Jeff summarized their success with, "We've had three big ideas at Amazon that we've stuck with for 18 years, and they're the reason we're successful: Put the customer first. Invent. And be patient," and Jeff has broken these elements of success down further:

1. **Regret minimization**: Jeff poetically intoned at one graduation commencement event that, "When you are in the thick of things, you can get confused by small stuff," he said later: "I knew when I was 80 that I would never, for example, think about why I walked away from my 1994 Wall Street bonus right in the middle of the year at the worst possible time; that kind of thing just isn't something you worry about when you're eighty years old— At the same time, I knew that I might sincerely regret not having participated in this thing called the Internet that I thought was going to be a revolutionizing event; when I thought about it that way…it was incredibly easy to make the decision."

Perhaps the chief motto of Jeff Bezos' life would be to live without regret. In his numerous graduation commencement speech opportunities, he has spoken to the newly minted professionals of America and intoned to please seek the difficult path. Jeff has warned them against that private place in one's head, where you are most accountable, and he has told students not to let it be darkened with might have been.

One of the chief reasons Jeff decided to leave New York to found Amazon was that he had just finished the book *Remains of the Day*. A story about a man, working as a butler, who was reflecting on the choices he had made professionally and personally throughout his war career in the United Kingdom— and the according fallout. The character from Kazuo Ishiguro's work experienced painful regret over not taking adequate risk. Jeff took this book's sentiments to heart: This regret minimization theory was to develop and follow Jeff throughout his entire career and to become one of the pieces of advice he most stridently tries to instill in those that ask him about how to succeed in the business world. He describes his choice to leave a comfortable career as experimental— Jeff emphasizes the need to be experimental in adopting a company, but the greatest experiment he may ever have conducted was with uprooting his own life from New York to be a pioneer in the e-commerce trade. To this day, when Jeff Bezos makes a list of important reads, he includes the work of *Remains of the Day*.

2. **Every day is day one:** "There is so much stuff that has yet to be invented; there's so much new that's going to happen; people don't have any idea yet how impactful the internet is going to be and that this is still Day 1 in such a big way," and Jeff says that "Day Two is stasis; followed by irrelevance; followed by excruciating, painful decline. Followed by death. And that is why it is always Day One at Amazon."

In other words, Jeff's beliefs stay at the Day 1, the startup mentality, or die a death of irrelevance. The Day One policy permeates everything that Jeff does from his philanthropy measures, to innovative ambitions— even his work with the homeless is titled with this philosophy. This core belief sprung from Jeff's experience as he saw the tremendous growth of the internet— and knew that it was only the beginning. Jeff saw the potential and realized that for e-commerce— this was Day One. He continues to encourage his employees to regard Amazon as in startup mode.

A terrific example of Jeff's commitment to his "Day 1" mentality is his venture into grocery retail. In a bizarrely cyclical turn of events Amazon had to face down corporate giants like Walmart after his purchase of Whole Foods. Amazon began a whole new fight over territory when it purchased the Whole Foods Market in 2017. These court battles must have felt like deja vu following his legal battles with the Riggio brothers of Barnes and Noble. Amazon purchased Whole Foods for a whopping $13.7 billion dollars. Jeff had been pushing to break into the supermarket field for a number of years. This purchase would mean that his online market place was once more facing down giants like Walmart that dominated the industry for a generation. Prime members enjoy discounts with Whole Foods. It is working to integrate its shipping and production methods with the Amazon model. It seems mildly poetic that Jeff's work has been compared to Sam Walton's pioneering of the Walmart model.

It is a testament to how quickly this evolution of progress has occurred that the founders of some of the organizations Amazon has deposed have not even begun to enjoy their own conquests before Amazon unseated them. Specifically, the toppling of the Riggio brothers of Barnes and Noble. And the suits bought by Walmart, which feels its throne is precarious— although the Walton family can hardly have settled down in the very few years that have passed since they revolutionized the mom-and-pop approach to groceries.

3. **Keep adapting**: "Because, you know, resilience --

if you think of it in terms of the Gold Rush, then you'd be pretty depressed right now because the last nugget of gold would be gone, but the good thing is, with innovation, there isn't a last nugget: Every new thing creates two new questions and two new opportunities."

Jeff is always planning for the next nugget of intellectual gold. Sometimes he strikes a vein: Kindle, Amazon brick and mortar stores, Amazon's speaker — Echo, ventures into grocery chains, media outlets, and the mind-boggling plethora that has become the "Everything Store" are testaments to Jeff's perpetual drive to keep re-inventing. But adaptation in the face of failure makes Jeff's work particularly impressive. His intellectual mines have "gone bust" on a number of occasions: The Fire phone, online auctioneering, and the staggering funds lost during the Dotcom bust prove that it takes courage to adapt in the face of setbacks.

In a fascinating recent economic shift, Jeff moved to open the first physical Amazon book store in Seattle. The store featured Amazon electronics alongside physical books. This ironic shift answered some of the criticism that Amazon has received for the retrenching of local books stores amongst the online book buying craze. Like so many other financial moves, this proved to be highly successful, and there are now fifteen Amazon book store locations available nationwide.

Interestingly, one Chicago based Amazon investor seemingly accidentally released Jeff's intention to open up hundreds of other similar physical outlets. This puzzled many Amazon watchers, but one news outlet reasoned that "Retail locations will help Amazon win on delivery. Retail stores could double as product pickup locations, distribution warehouses," and eventually, they could serve as, "drone airports from which products are flown to nearby homes and businesses." This source anticipates Jeff overcoming drone legal hurdles and using the physical store locations to provide still faster drop off times to customers.

Jeff announced in 2013, for the first time, that he was ambitious to begin delivery of products through the use of drones. Jeff's drone made its first delivery in the United Kingdom— it had delivered the customer's package in an incredible thirteen minutes. He faced legislative pushback in the United States but continues to work toward this goal.

4. **Customer care**: "If there's one reason we have done better than our peers in the Internet space over the last six years, it is because we have focused like a laser on customer experience, and that really does matter, I think, in any business; it certainly matters online, where word-of-mouth is so very, very powerful."

Jeff Bezos made his fortune in just five years: they call it the Internet Bonanza, as in he's just rounding up money like the head cowboy of cyberspace. During his finance arc, he clocked a three hundred- and ninety-seven percent increase in the value of his stock. The secret: "We don't make money when we sell things — We make money when we help customers make purchasing decisions." He's saying that making buying easy for consumers makes Amazon wealthy.

He reminds his employees that when customers have a bad experience, they don't just tell one person; they tell five thousand friends. At meetings, he is famous for leaving one chair empty — this chair symbolizes a spot held for the customer — whom he considers the most important person in the room. He says that part of having that lasting company is the ability to maintain authentic customer care. Jeff summarized their mentality toward customers with, "We are not competitor obsessed, we are customer obsessed. We start with the customer, and we work backward," and repeats that, "If you do build a great experience, customers tell each other about that. Word-of-mouth is very powerful." Jeff warns that stockholders that have invested in Amazon hold only paper wealth — sustainable for as long as their company continues to treat customers well.

5. **Take risks**: "Sometimes you've got to dive in and take the chance that you might fail; the worst thing about any business is that you might inevitably fall down. The good part about this is that you've found out what doesn't work and that you have only one direction to go; taking a risk isn't about failing, but it is about living up to the ideals that business is built upon: In order to get something you've never had you have to be willing to do something you've never done before — Taking a risk means going all in and hoping for the best while at times expecting the worst."

Jeff says that it is incredibly hard to get people to take bold risks — He finds that most people are concerned with the financial fashions of that day. There may be no stronger example of this than Jeff's very first hire, Shel Kaphlan. Shel Kaphlan is considered the unnamed co-founder of Amazon with Jeff. Shel was bolder than most— he moved to Amazon from California after just a breakfast meeting. Shel was required to buy a portion of Amazon's stock at the outset, and he was invited to invest further. However, he declined the opportunity even though he has shared that at the time he had the savings to do so. He said it wasn't worth the risk. That invitation and that investment today represents millions of dollars in lost opportunity.

If Shel had invested $1,000 when Amazon went public in May 1997, his initial investment would be worth $1,362,000, today. As the earliest founder, he had the opportunity to make even more from that initial investment. Over the course of 1994, Jeff had sixty meetings— asking his friends and family to take a risk with his new company. A whopping 38 of them turned him down. That's almost two thirds. The initial twenty-two investors that included Jeff's family and friends each got one percent of Bezos' firm in return their investment of fifty thousand dollars- - that is an astonishing 14 million per cent return now makes each of those original shares worth a minimum of seven billion dollars (depending on whether they invested more than that the minimum.) Jeff still has contact with some of the people that passed on his invitation to invest. He says it's something of a study in human nature to watch them process their lost opportunity: some of them can't even speak about it; it's just too painful.

6. **Be Frugal**: "I think frugality drives innovation— just like other constraints do; one of the only ways to get out of a tight box is to invent your way out."

In discussions about being frugal, Jeff talks to Amazon's workers about Muga— which is the Japanese concept of waste. Jeff has told his employees they are waging a guerrilla war on wasteful spending. In the '90s, he was mocked for his frugal attitude. Today, when addressing or sizing up leaders at Amazon, Jeff uses the resourcefulness that frugality breeds as a ph scale. Even though Jeff is committed to having Amazon act like a startup, he refused to engage in the current culture of startups. He says companies shouldn't obsess with what's shiny: no company ever stays that way. For reference, all Amazon desks are still made out of doors— reflecting Jeff's initial commitment to founding the company economically; employees describe this phenomenon as a hallowed part of their corporate culture, like Noah building the ark. In fact, executives grumble about the particle board desks splintering and catching on their clothes, but they have learned to carry sandpaper with them to the office — to sand down their own desks because Jeff is truly committed to being frugal.

Externally, Jeff faced pressure to provide fashionable fringe benefits like break room drinks, paid leave for people that had recently acquired a new puppy (pawternity leave), or vacation flex time. Amazon's attitude toward business travel also makes it unique — executives, anyone that flies for corporate events or meetings are required to chip in themselves for flight bump ups. Jeff says that common sense measures like these help keep costs down for their consumers. However, he did allow employees in certain venues to bring their dogs to work with them. Doubtless, this concession was to Seattle's warm attitude toward dog ownership.

7. **Pick a Good Name**: "Many customers want something that flashes out at them and grabs their attention: A lackluster name won't attract many consumers and will likely serve to push your product into the dark corner of the retail market where few consumers, if any, ever look; to add some

pizzazz to your business you want to settle on a name that will inspire a sense of wonder and interest in your customer and actually get them interested in seeing what you have to sell — If they will bank on your name just enough to take a look, then you might just have a chance."

Jeff may not place his confidence in advertising, but he does believe in the power of a good name for the company. It may seem like a small detail for someone consumed by the rigors of turning their life upside down to be part of a startup, but early on Jeff invested time in his choosing his names for Amazon and later for his space venture, Blue Origin. Blue Origin is a ringing reference to space colonization originating from the blue planet, Earth. However, the genesis of the name Amazon is not as easily determined.

In the beginning, Amazon went through a number of name changes. In tribute to his love of space and once more to Star Trek, Jeff thought about calling the fledgling organization "make it so." He also had considered calling it Cadabra — like the organization was providing magic. Amazon was actually incorporated under this initial name. However, this second name died a quick death after Jeff's lawyer heard the word cadaver over the phone, and Jeff decided that was not the connotation he wanted for his fledgling company. They briefly considered calling their new site relentless.com, which may have spoken to Jeff's internal drive. He got feedback that it sounded perhaps a little sinister for a book retailer, but to this day that web address still routes customers to the Amazon site. Eventually, Jeff settled on naming the new organization Amazon. He had been perusing the "A" section of the dictionary —- websites were still listed alphabetically, and he felt this would give them a competitive edge. He named it for what he perceived as the endless river of South America, with its multitude of branching streams. He wanted to create, "The Earth's Biggest Book Store," tagline through Amazon; he was looking for the name to reflect the vastness of their intent for their company. "This is not only the largest river in the world; it's many times larger than the next biggest river. It blows all other rivers away," Bezos recounted to his new team. And so, the company name Amazon was born.

8. **Business growth**: "There are two ways to extend a business: Take inventory of what you're good at and extend out from your skills, or determine what your customers need and work backward— even if it requires learning new skills; Kindle is an example of working backward."

Jeff adopted both strategies when he developed the Kindle — Amazon had made book buying easier, faster, and far more affordable for consumers, but with the Kindle, Jeff was set to revolutionize the books themselves. In 2007, in time for the Christmas season, Amazon introduced the Kindle reader — it was an electronic device that was capable of holding hundreds of digitized books. Initially, developers had called the product Fiona — a reference to a science fiction book where an engineer gifts an interactive reader to his daughter, Fiona. However, Jeff went with the name Kindle because it sounded as though they were going to start a fire. And start a fire they did. Readers could now have a virtual library with them wherever they went. Jeff had surpassed his own vision of creating an online book store that could hold more than was physically possible. Now, the average person could have on hand more books than should have been physically available to them.

Jeff innovated the new devices, keeping his customers' comfort in mind. The backlighting of Kindles was designed to reduce the eye strain that readers experienced when using their laptops to read. Books were deeply, almost shockingly affordable at $9.99, and could be purchased wirelessly. Jeff had the new Kindle use Whisper-sync tech that enabled readers to pick up where they left off on a separate device. This revolution in information access was the most dramatic usurping of traditional reading since Gutenberg had invented his press in 1468. Sales increased with the introduction of Kindle. They benefitted Amazon by a thirty-eight percent escalation in book sales. The success of the Kindle also reinvented the image of Amazon for investors and the public. Jeff had achieved a brand face that reflected Amazon as one of the economy's leading tech pioneers. He says that "To get something new done you have to be stubborn and focused, to the point that others might find unreasonable."

9. **Corporate Culture**: "When I interview people, I tell them: 'You can work long, hard, or smart, but at Amazon.com you can't choose two out of three."

Jeff has developed a culture that some have said is certainly not warm and fuzzy. He has extremely high standards for those that he partners with. In fact, some have described Amazon's workplace as painful, burn and churn, and as "gladiator culture." However, despite the sometimes-scathing reviews, Amazon's own employees have come to Jeff's defense of Amazon's corporate culture. They have described the high of working at an extraordinary pace that accomplishes the impossible. Jeff says that you can't buy loyalty. However, Jeff says you can create an atmosphere where workers are there for more than just a paycheck; they are there because they believe in the vision. Despite the rigors of Amazon's corporate culture and his commitment to frugality, Amazon takes care of its employees. Amazon employees post reviews that the business model reflects an effort to make sure its workers have a decent wage, and Amazon's corporate culture invests in general wellbeing.

For a man that describes a company's brand as what is said when you aren't there, these outside reviews are high praise. One Amazon insider remarked that "they pay pretty well — above the average. Their frugality does not apply to salary. Honestly, I think they try to save the money to pay us better and get a better return to the shareholders." In response to yet another outreach poll to consumers, Jeff raised Amazon's minimum wage for its workers up to fifteen dollars an hour. This raise impacts two hundred and fifty thousand of its workers — and will also be reflected in the wages of its one hundred thousand seasonal staff members. Additionally, Amazon experimented with thirty-hour work weeks for employees — who made seventy-five percent of their usual pay but were entitled to full benefits.

10. **Motivation**: "I think one thing I find very motivating — and I think this is probably a very common form of motivation or cause of motivation is (that) I love people counting on me, ... today it's so easy to be motivated because we have millions of customers counting on us at Amazon.com: We've got thousands of investors counting on us; and we're a team of thousands of employees all counting on each other: That's fun."

If Jeff is motivated by having other people rely on him, then he has a lot to get him up in the morning. Jeff has a family that he invests in at the beginning of each day — including his three sons and adopted daughter. Additionally, Amazon can now boast over six hundred thousand employees. Jeff has also made the homeless crisis of his new hometown, Seattle, a philanthropic priority. This city is home to one of the country's most significant homelessness crises. He responded with a billion-dollar investment into aiding the issue. Finally, Jeff's customer service obsessed metric leaves him feeling personally responsible for the consumer's wellbeing.

11. **Dealing with Challenges**: "When the world changes around you, and when it changes against you, what used to be a tail wind is now a headwind — you have to lean into that and figure out what to do — because complaining isn't a strategy."

Jeff's singular combination of adaptability and commitment to treating each day like it's Amazon's first day prepare him to meet challenges with unusual grace. Specifically, When Amazon was a fledgling startup, they were looking to save money with how they acquired their books: Ingram's was their Seattle supplier. Jeff had known that was who he wanted to work with before he even moved to the city — That supplier had been a motivating factor in their transition from New York. However, Ingrams required purchasers to order a minimum of ten books for every single purchase. For an organization that was operating out of a garage, this number was daunting and unrealistic. Jeff came up with a plan; he had found a loophole in Ingram's supply system. They would order the book they needed and then nine copies of a deeply obscure book on plant foliage. That plant book was forever out of stock, and so they were able to avoid the extra book penalty.

12: **Think Big**: "Thinking small is a self-fulfilling prophecy— Leaders create and communicate a bold direction that inspires results: They think differently and look around corners for ways to serve customers."

Bezos tells reporters that his motto is "gradatim ferociter," which is Latin for "step-by-step courageously." He says that the biggest oak tree comes from an acorn, and that process takes time— it's step by step. With characteristic optimism, he's implying that to plant an acorn you have to at least be hoping for an oak tree.

Reportedly, "Almost since the beginning of Amazon.com's remarkable rise, Bezos has been characterized as yet another fuzzy-cheeked geek who lucked into an IPO…" Many called Jeff, "an uninspired financial technician with a good but not very original idea about distributing goods over the Internet, who would soon be, "Amazon.toast." The report continued that, "It's a characterization Bezos' competitors have found costly. They may also have missed that, in focusing on the consumer in a way few web entrepreneurs can match— he is actually trying to transform the world."

Despite outside skepticism, from the beginning, Jeff's ambition to transform the world was successful. His ambition worked. It worked beyond anything Jeff or anyone else could ever have dared to hope for. By the end of August 1995 (the first month after launching Amazon) they were doing twenty thousand dollars a week in sales.

At the end of the first seventeen months, Amazon had done well over five hundred thousand dollars in business. Jeff had the oak tree he had been hoping for. And they kept climbing. By the end of 1996 Amazon had over a hundred employees and had done 15.7 million dollars in sales. This was only a little over two years from launching their online book store from the chilly garage with its unreliable electricity.

13. **Professional Conflict**: "Have Backbone; Disagree and Commit — Leaders are obligated to respectfully challenge decisions when they disagree, even when doing so is uncomfortable or exhausting; leaders have conviction and are tenacious… They do not compromise for the sake of social cohesion. Once a decision is determined, they commit

wholly."

Even early on, Jeff demonstrated backbone and commitment as he faced down fearsome competitors. By its third year Jeff was ready to take the company public, but the infamous Riggio brothers of Barnes and Noble were making good on their threat to sue Amazon. Accordingly, they fought back against Jeff. They brought a suit against Amazon for its tagline: "The Earth's Largest Book Store." They circulated that they had twice the number of books of any other book store out there. Jeff wanted to take the company public as the next step in their growth. On May 15, 1997, Amazon took the leap and went public. Going public meant that Amazon had transformed into a company worth three hundred million dollars. Jeff warned investors that he expected the company to be operating in the red for a while to come.

Playing especially dirty, Barnes and Noble brought their suit as Jeff was seeking to take the company public. There is a week-long period of silence when a company is becoming an IPO. Jeff couldn't talk to the press about Amazon's state of affairs. Never one to fall behind or miss an opportunity, Jeff adapted. He changed Amazon's tagline from, "The Earth's Biggest Book Store" to "Books, Music, and More." This adaptation was a reflection of the fact that Jeff had already expanded Amazon's sales to include the burgeoning market of online music. It was also a power stroke because the Barnes brothers were now holding a suit against what has been called an economic phantom. Jeff had stood firm, and they eventually settled out of court.

However, with a further mark of aggression, Barnes and Noble had quickly developed their own competing website to try to subdue Amazon's sales but to little avail: Amazon was holding eighty-five percent of the online book sales market, while Barnes and Noble was only able to maintain an eleven percent share. This is especially impressive considering that Barnes and Noble represented Jeff's closest competition in the online book sales market. In the near future, these organizations may no longer even be considered a source of competition for Amazon's sales.

Jeff summarizes inner-Amazon conflict with: "Recognize true misalignment issues early and escalate them immediately. Sometimes teams have different objectives and fundamentally different views. They are not aligned — no amount of discussion, no number of meetings will resolve that deep misalignment. Without escalation, the default dispute resolution mechanism for this scenario is exhaustion: Whoever has more stamina carries the decision," says Bezos, who adds: "'You've worn me down' is an awful decision-making process. It's slow and de-energizing." He says to, "Go for quick escalation instead."

14. **Experiment**: "If you double the number of experiments you do per year— you're going to double your inventiveness."

This seems like an easy thing for one of the most successful men in history to say, but Jeff says that he has made billions of dollars of mistakes throughout his career— he warns those entering the realm of experimental business that they are facing the fact that it is very easy to have a concept— but he tells listeners that turning that idea into reality in the face of failures is the true challenge.

eBay also presented itself as a stiff competitor. At one time, Jeff had built his own auction site to try battle for the market share that eBay was presenting. Unfortunately, this endeavor failed. Reportedly, Jeff tried to engage with the founders of eBay to collude. The new founders were apparently put off to some extent by Jeff's famous laugh and no agreement was reached. So, Jeff built his own auction site. It was partially unsuccessful because customers were used to the polished efficiency that provided their products— Amazon's new auction house made customers feel like they were experiencing a second-hand store, compared to the traditional model. However, comically, Jeff was its very best customer. At one point, he purchased a full Ice Age cave bear skeleton for himself— placing it in one of Amazon's facilities with a label that read, "please do not feed the bear." Even in the midst of a challenging atmosphere, Jeff insisted on keeping a sense of humor.

15. **Move with speed**: "Most decisions are easily reversible— Many decisions are not life and death and can be easily reversed— If a decision can be reversed with relatively little pain or suffering, don't waste much time. Make a decision, and then change course if it ended up being wrong."

Bezos says that you should make a decision with thirty percent of the information you currently have but act like you have the seventy percent of the information that you would like to have— In other words, if you wait to have all the facts then you will probably never make a decision. And as a professional, you will definitely be missing a lot of financial opportunities. He emphasizes that even counting mistakes, most decisions can be mitigated — The goal is to move quickly on potential investment ventures that would otherwise be irredeemably irretrievable. He summarizes his successfully quick method as, "Most decisions should probably be made with somewhere around 70% of the information you wish you had. If you wait for 90%, in most cases, you're probably being slow. Plus, either way, you need to be good at quickly recognizing and correcting bad decisions. If you're good at course correcting, being wrong may be less costly than you think, whereas being slow is going to be expensive for sure."

For example, even when Jeff faced taking a hit, he moved with speed on financial progress. In 2014 Jeff experienced one of the few setbacks Amazon would know after it survived the fallout of the Dotcom bust. He introduced the Fire phone, which unfortunately was an economic failure. Amazon found itself unable to compete with Apple's iPhone or with the Android. The company took a one hundred and seventy million dollar hit and ceased production on the Fire phone that same year, but Jeff really took this hit in stride. The company lost millions of dollars on this venture… but with characteristic humor, Jeff said, "If you think that's a big failure, we're working on much bigger failures right now — and I am not kidding," he told one media outlet, "Some of them are going to make the Fire Phone look like a tiny little blip." Once more his confidence paid off when two years after the Fire phone flopped, Jeff introduced the Echo, which made Amazon a powerful corner in the electronics market.

16. **Build a Culture:** "Find a way to create something unique; most businesses simply continue an existing culture— adding to it much as a child would pack snow onto a fort during the winter to stabilize its walls: Don't just add onto something else, create your own culture by building up a business or something similar that is its own entity… Before Amazon, online purchasing was almost non-existent; now, legions of consumers would look at you funny if you asked what this service is."

One of the best examples of Jeff's impact on culture is his development of the futuristic electronic personal assistant, Alexa. The quiet infiltration into American homes was surreal— even a few years ago this tech would have astounded Amazon watchers, but Alexa has entered American culture with both speed and finesse:

In one account, a lady had a surreal experience as she sat in Washington D.C. at a brunch held in a friend's home— Their host's four-year-old daughter was playing in the next room, while they ate. She heard as the little girl commanded Alexa to play her favorite nursery rhyme— the child would make requests at random, with Alexa adapting to the child's whims. From the next room, her father intoned to his daughter, Ivy, tell Alexa to turn it down. The four-year-old looked up from her toys and imperiously told Alexa to turn down the volume on the nursery rhyme. Alexa had entered their home as an ever-ready personal assistant; she is the futuristic product— Jeff's virtual assistant that operates off of his Echo platform. She was readily embraced for her "skills" as a natural part of the family home: reading nursery rhymes to the children, doing their bedtime stories, summing up the day's news, keeping appointments, aiding in meditation routines, reciting cookbook recipes… she didn't just impact American culture, she helped develop it.

17. **Reputation Matters**: "You don't have to be a crusader for any one cause— but standing for something such as quality and assurance that your products will always be

just what the consumer wants is a good start in business—
Your word means a lot when you conduct your own business,
and should you be able to stand behind that, then customers
will rally to you in order to give you their business; *a business
that can't or won't stand behind its own guarantees is one that is
destined for obscurity."*

Jeff asserts that building a reputation for a business is like building one for a person— he cautions professionals that your brand is what people say when you aren't in the room. It's that word-of-mouth, customer trust that Jeff has based much of his success and expansion for Amazon on. He emphasizes that customer loyalty is something to be cultivated— Jeff's strict adherence to his early principles founded and then guided Amazon into staggering success for the last quarter of a century. In the beginning, Jeff opened Amazon without alerting the media. Jeff has even noted his suspicion of business models that centrally rely on their ability to market to succeed.

One very keen story illustrating Jeff's commitment to a reputation for good customer service was the conflict surrounding the first commercial filmed for Amazon's Kindle. The commercial featured a matador and a charging bull.

Apparently, the entire staff laughed at the depiction— but after it finished, Jeff went up to the dark screen and said— I know it's cute, I know lots of people with think that bull bit is funny, but that commercial had the customer getting hurt, and we have to protect the customer. For Jeff, taking care of the consumer is no jest.

18. **Communication**: "We don't do PowerPoint (or any other slide-oriented) presentations at Amazon: Instead, we write narratively structured 6-page memos... We silently read one at the beginning of each meeting in a kind of study hall; not surprisingly, the quality of these memos varies widely— Some have the clarity of angels singing; they are brilliant and thoughtful and set up the meeting for high-quality discussion; sometimes they come in at the other end of the spectrum."

Jeff has a very curious corporate communication mentality. In American culture, free and prolific communication isn't just seen as necessary, it is almost worshipped, and the bullet point summary style that PowerPoint facilitates has almost a ritualistic standard. However, Jeff requires six-page memos for meetings, that Jeff says should take a week to write. They read them at the beginning of the meeting: "We read in the room; just like high school kids, executives will bluff their way through the meeting as if they've read the memo. So, you have to carve out time, so everyone has actually read the memo -- they are not just pretending," he said. But he limits communication in other ways— he only meets with Amazon's investors for a shocking six hours a year. He's busy making Amazon a success, instead of courting their funds.

He asserts that over-communication is a sign of failure. And he has fine-tuned brevity: One of the worst emails an employee can get from Jeff is just one single character: "?" in the subject line. When an Amazon employee gets one of the dreaded question mark emails, that single character is described as a ticking time bomb. The recipient has a matter of hours to explain why the issue occurred in the first place and to find a solution for the issue to present to Jeff.

He also has the catchy two-pizza-rule for meetings. Jeff says that no meeting should ever have so many people that it could not easily feed all the attendants with just two pizzas. So, no Amazon meeting should ever have more than ten people in attendance. He asserts that this two-pizza rule keeps the company from falling into group think.

19. **Leadership**: "They (leaders) act on behalf of the entire company, beyond just their own team; they never say, "that's not my job."

There is a level of humility and a servant leadership perspective that enables a true leader to see what needs to be done and do it, according to Jeff. Jeff would know. He is famous for personally responding to customer's emails.

Customers can email the Amazon CEO, personally. A famous anecdote recounts that one of Jeff's premier innovations in online shopping involved email confirmations. When Amazon's customers make a purchase an email confirming their item, payment, and shipping details quickly follows. This innovation in tech customer service was an element of the ultimate success of Amazon. Jeff's implementation of email confirmations and customer book reviews put Amazon far ahead of the curve on online book sales — Jeff noticed a pattern of consumers complaining to him about the email confirmation service. They had been purchasing personal items through Amazon and felt humiliated at receiving emails about the products to their inboxes. Jeff nearly ground the multi-million email process to a halt over a few customers' concerns.

Some former employees have felt disgruntled at Jeff's attitude that no one is above attending to the details of the company. One former Amazon engineer that left to go work for Google, Steve Yegge, garnered attention grumbling about the decor at Amazon, the food, and their pay. He also said that he was required to do dingy jobs at times. He called Jeff: Dread Pirate Bezos, "who issues mandates that cause people to scramble like ants being pounded with a rubber mallet," according to Forbes. However, Yegge praised Bezos' nimble business model, his ability to push massive changes through Amazon, the initiatives that led to Amazon Web Services. Yegge says that even tech powerhouse Google hasn't been able to react so quickly with its own Web services.

20. **Process is Messy**: "When a company comes up with an idea, it's a messy process: There's no 'aha' moment."

Jeff emphasizes that there is no ability to quantify Amazon's success in a neat package. Chalk it up to humility or believe that the man is mysterious, but he says that development, economic evolution is a very messy business. For a man that declared that progress is messy, he also emphasized that the best approach to making a success amongst this chaos is to be clinical, to approach figures with an experimental mindset.

As proof of this mess, it may be noted that there were small scale rebellions in Amazon's production houses. One employee rode the warehouse package conveyor all through the facility. Another comical account is that of a now ex-employee.

The Amazon warehouse worker would show up at the start of his shift and leave at the end of it, but they had discovered that he never logged any hours in between. It took at least a week for anyone to discover what was going on. Unbelievably, the employee had tunneled out a den inside a huge pile of empty wooden pallets. Completely out of view, he had used Amazon products to make a bed and ripped pictures from Amazon books to line his make-shift bunker walls. He had stolen Amazon food to snack on. When the employee was later discovered, he was — not surprisingly — fired.

Chapter 6 - Make It So: Jeff Bezos' Philanthropic Life

"Nearly all men can stand adversity, but if you want to test a man's character: give him power." – President Abraham Lincoln

The year was 1864, and Abraham Lincoln had just been re-elected President. The American Civil War was raging, and Sherman's March to the Sea was to burn its way across the landscape of the nation. It was the great upheaval of mankind — that would bear the standard of freedom for the West and re-define the human experience, setting humanity on equal footing for the first time in its ten-thousand-year existence. The following century, born out of the blood of embattled brothers, ushered in a gentler era; it cradled the wonders of the Industrial Revolution, and at its turn, Victorian Era inventors would see such incredible progress that they remarked that, "everything that could be invented had been invented."

It was one century before Jeff Bezos was to be born; symmetrically, the year Jeff was born the culture waring through another deeply divided era — 1964 was the year of the radical, the year of great progress in the Civil Rights movement— the Summer after he was born was called Freedom Summer: That year, at thirty-five, Dr. Martin Luther King Jr. became the youngest ever recipient of the Nobel Peace Prize, and it was the year the momentous Civil Rights Act was signed into law. This progress also came at a terrible price - three Freedom Summer riders were found in a dam. They had been murdered for participating in the protest.

The ensuing decades of change would boost their own economic revolution with the dawn of the internet. At the turn of this century, only a few years after the internet's birth, American society had become utterly dependent on it. They even feared a crash they nicknamed Y2K. Many feared computers would come to a grinding halt—knocking off electricity, water, basic communication, and many other social fundamentals that the internet had quickly adapted to hosting. There was widespread building of bunkers, food caches became a matter of polite conversation, and society's great fear was that the millennia would see a dark dawn. The most fearful dug underground bunkers, and there they waited for the end. None of these fears were fulfilled. Sinks still ran, ketchup was still immediately available, and the lights shone on to reveal a culture breathing a sigh of relief.

It is this sigh of relief that is fascinating. How did the internet revolutionize and become an indispensable part of society —

such that its darkening was seen as a cultural doom, all in the time it takes an 18-year-old to pass through college? Children born around the same time that the internet was labored into the public's grasp, were still learning to read. But the infantile internet, in the same number of years, had already become foundational to society. Men like Jeff Bezos are extraordinary because they taught the internet to walk. What makes Jeff a leader among even these argonauts was that he taught it to speak. Society was immediately in awe of the information access that the newly vocal internet provided, but Bezos' entrepreneurial oracle intones that these are but the internet age's first words.

Jeff has utilized the infrastructure from his multi-tier internet boomtown as a foundation that supports many other progressive endeavors: his space colonization platform, Blue Origin, his efforts to promote free speech, with his purchase of the *Washington Post*, and his variety of philanthropic endeavors:

Blue Origin:

Fascinatingly, intellectual ages dawn and darken with a

humanoid symphonic quality — there was the multi-competitor race to invent the television, the age of great classical music — the age of baroque paintings with Caravaggio and his followers: There seems to be an unexplained harmonic unity in the geniuses of each age. The space race is in its second movement, but perhaps the strongest measures are being set by men like Jeff Bezos: Jeff's foresight is the genesis of his space colonization project: Blue Origin. Blue Origin's mission is to make space flight economical for every individual and to facilitate extra-earth space colonization.

Blue Origin is a very beautiful vision to be incepted in an era of dread — Specifically, Jeff was born into a decade that predicted the "Population Bomb." It was rumored that the human population was following a trajectory that could not be supported by the current food supply. Books predicted mass starvation; parents were encouraged to stop having children that would be born into a cruel world. But Jeff's vision is a testament to the innovative and hopeful spirit of mankind. In a chromatic discussion, Jeff says that the extension of humanity is the extension of its genius. In other words, as humanity grows so proportionally grows the number of musicians, scientists, writers, inventors, ballerinas, and painters. Space colonization and resource harvesting facilitate these wunderkinds; these wonder children for the betterment of earth and the greater universe. Jeff says that through space, "We have the resources to build rooms for a trillion humans in this solar system, and when we have a trillion humans, we'll have a thousand Einsteins and a thousand Mozarts. It will be a way more interesting place to live."

In 2064, what will they say about Jeff Bezos space venture? His investment as king of commerce, the information age, and the great space venture is the infrastructure from which future generations will continue to defy that there is nothing left to invent. They will stand on Jeff Bezos' shoulders and continue the great experiment of the human existence. Perhaps, their act of the defiant march of knowledge will take place on another planet.

Sardonically, Jeff laughs that you can't build a giant space company in your dorm room… well not yet anyway. This quixotic remark is a reference to Jeff's commitment to using his resources to build the infrastructure of space conquest. He believes that his work with Amazon makes him a lottery winner— and he wants to invest his winnings in the next generation's ability to be space-bound: "Of course humans like to explore, and we should: There's nothing wrong with that. But it's more than that; it's essential for your children and your children's children."

Listening to Jeff discuss his intentions for space exploration and colonization gives one a sense that life on another planet is already almost palpable to him. Through his telescopic view of human nature, he spies practical issues future moon dwellers will face and charmingly details their resolution: "The Moon Village concept has a nice property in that it basically just says, 'Look, everybody builds their own lunar outpost, but let's do it close to each other.' That way... you can go over to the European Union lunar outpost and say, 'I'm out of eggs. What have you got?'" Jeff also feels that human beings, at least at the beginning of colonization will naturally want to remain rather close to their home planet: "When we build our own colonies, we can do them in near-Earth vicinity— because people are going to want to come back to Earth. Very few people, for a long time, anyway, are going to want to abandon Earth altogether." Interestingly, this quote implies he foresees the possibility of a human existence entirely apart from its origin.

Recognizing the unparalleled prosperity of this present age, Jeff says that one of the greatest challenges to the space endeavor is humanity's current comfort. He notes that at the current growth trajectory of energy consumption, one would need to cover the earth in solar panels to continue the advancing arc. It isn't just the ability to sustain life on earth that concerns Jeff— Just as he built Amazon with a focus on building a company that lasts, he endeavors to incept a space commerce that has bones to serve future ages. With possibly some chagrin, he notes past efforts have certainly not been directed towards a fundamentally enduring space endeavor. Particularly, the Apollo missions, he says were not purposed to endure— "The Apollo program certainly had no real commercial value; it was done for very different reasons and, I think, very good reasons for the time: It's an extraordinary achievement of mankind, but it wasn't sustainable." Jeff would know. He personally helped fund the retrieval of remnants of this mission from the ocean floor. Jeff poetically remarked that retrieval mission, "We've seen an underwater wonderland – an incredible sculpture garden of twisted F-1 engines that tells the story of a fiery and violent end; one that serves testament to the Apollo program".

Washington Post:

Perhaps one of the greater altruistic investments of Jeff's career is his momentum with sustaining news outlets; he has contributed significant funds to free press measures. However, his most astonishing foray into the world of media was his surprising purchase of the *Washington Post*.

In a discussion of his purchase of the *Washington Post*, Jeff exclaimed over his new acquisition, "Important institutions like the *Washington Post* have an essence, they have a heart, they have a core…" Jeff continued that, "And if you wanted that to change, you'd be crazy. That's part of what this place is; it's part of what makes it so special." Jeff says that the *Washington Post* is a swashbuckling sort of outlet. He likes that it swaggers.

In 2013, Jeff Bezos made headlines as the new owner of the *Washington Post*. He purchased the heralded news outlet for two hundred and fifty million dollars. Excited Amazon watchers are particularly attentive to this purchase because of what it may signify about the newspaper industry as a whole. The newspaper industry has struggled to adapt to the internet age since its birth in the nineties — who better to reform an e-commerce reluctant industry than Jeff Bezos?

This purchase of the *Washington Post* may be the strongest example of Jeff's advice to fellow businessmen to "Follow your heart, not your head." Jeff reasoned to listeners that, "Too often your head will argue that caution is needed — that you must act in a way that will keep you safe and secure." He continued that, "Your heart will tell you to go for it more often than not, relying more on instinct than experience to take charge of life and do what is necessary. In order to strike a proper balance between the two it is often better to lead with the heart and allow the head to operate as it will by adapting and evolving to a continually changing environment."

Jeff is nothing if not a man of method— However, in a 2016 speech, he revealed that he didn't do any due diligence before he purchased the Washington Post. It is Jeff's deviation from his set character that makes this purchase an interesting hallmark in an already remarkable life. It demonstrates a fundamental commitment to free language, to the free press. He proclaimed that "Beautiful speech doesn't need protection, it's ugly speech that needs protection. We have these cultural norms that allow people to say really ugly things; you don't have to invite them to your dinner party, but you should let them say it."

In an after-purchase interview, Jeff assured the public and the staff of the *Washington Post* that he has great respect for the paper's legacy, and his fine-tuning will centrally involve tailoring the paper to its customers' needs— its staff reacted accordingly, with hope and optimism. However, there has been some bitter grumbling from other news sources. Other outlets have increasingly and steadily faced staff cuts and budget reductions, while the *Washington Post* is being guided in a totally different direction. Whatever the grumbling of other media outlets, the *Post's* staff says it has been business as usual at the paper, in general.

Essentially, Jeff's purchase of the *Washington Post* was a heartfelt decision. However, with his talents, Jeff may revolutionize the way that the news is consumed as fully as he has revolutionized the way that the globe embraced the Kindle's e-books. It's certainly an exciting market to watch.

A Modern Andrew Carnegie Philanthropist:

In one interesting anecdote, famous millionaire and philanthropist Andrew Carnegie of the Gilded Age once gave an audience to an angry young man. When the man was shown to seeing Carnegie, he told Carnegie that possessing such wealth was wrong— he should divide it up amongst the populace. Carnegie paused, then called in his private secretary. Turning to his secretary, he asked, "What am I worth?" The secretary promptly volunteered Carnegie's current net worth. Then, Carnegie asked his secretary, "How many people are there in the world?" His secretary again supplied the number — to which Carnegie said, please divide the two numbers. The secretary replied, "It comes to sixteen cents." Abruptly, Carnegie reached into his pocket and counted out sixteen cents on his desk. He turned back to the angry young man and handed him the change, and said, "There's yours. Now get out of my office."

In America there are two ways wealth is disbursed — philanthropically or it is passed down to one's heirs. Andrew Carnegie is responsible for the genesis of the philanthropic model of giving wealth to benefit society. He told the millionaires of his era in an article entitled, "The Gospel of Wealth," that they were morally bound to use their funds to better humanity — he said that, "Surplus wealth is a sacred trust which its possessor is bound to administer in his lifetime for the good of the community." His words and example reverberate throughout American culture to this day. Carnegie asserted that wealth wasn't about self-indulgence — giving had to be done wisely, in ways that sincerely aided those in need. He spent the end of his life trying to give away his vast fortune in cautious, thoughtful investments for the betterment of America. He is perhaps best remembered for his work with libraries. Across the United States, in small towns, throughout urban cityscapes, Carnegie's legacy is a perennial bouquet of 2,509 libraries he erected with his massive fortune.

Today, Jeff Bezos often has angered members of the public with his approach to philanthropy. However, these naysayers misunderstand his model of generosity. Jeff gives to humanity in the Carnegie model. First, his innovations in the availability of the written word strongly parallels Carnegie. The Kindle, the cheap price of e-books, the availability of audiobooks— all bare a strong resemblance to Carnegie's investment in other's ability to learn. Currently, Jeff is at work, dedicating himself to making textbooks as affordable and available to students as possible. He signed deals such as his cooperation with Wylie Publishers, which gave readers cheap access to vast amounts of digitized versions of works. This move angered publishers because they weren't getting a cut, but it aided readers and writers— which translates to soaring reading numbers. Literacy has a champion in lifelong reader Jeff Bezos.

Second, Jeff is a long-term thinker. His bet on e-commerce was eerily and reverberatingly accurate; his foresight allowed Amazon to be born. Once more, he has made a bet— this time his wager is on space resources. Market watchers would do well to pay attention: Jeff has waged his life's success in building an infrastructure for future generations to build on in space exploration.

Whatever the criticism he has faced, Jeff isn't shy— he often encourages others to remember that if you want to accomplish things in life, you must be prepared to face criticisms from others. Sometimes those individuals will mean well, and sometimes they won't. He says if you are going to do anything new or interesting than that is always going to mean a level of being misunderstood. That doesn't mean adopting an attitude of obstinance: Rather, Jeff says to listen and hear whether or not they are right in critiquing you. Even if they aren't correct, they may have said something true that can serve as a source of inspiration. However, Jeff says it takes backbone to stand by what's right— "If you decide, by the way, that the answer is no, (that those criticizing you are wrong) ... then no force in the world should be able to move you." This humility toward criticism spawned the presence of negative book reviews on Amazon's website, and this same framework gives Jeff the strength to withstand criticism, today.

Nevertheless, Jeff has also invested his wealth in a variety of other philanthropic outlets: He has given two billion dollars to aid the homeless of Seattle. He has donated ten million dollars to an organization dedicated to helping more veterans gain political office.

Jeff is also involved in "Plenty," which is a vertical farming effort. Vertical farming involves tiered farms that are located near urban developments. Produce is grown on stacked high rises; imagine a skyscraper, where each successive floor is devoted to plants. It's the concept of preventing urban sprawl applied to agriculture. The benefits of developing such tech are that their proximity to cities allows those citizens to have fresher commodities. It's better for the people, and the transportation costs are largely negated. This style of farming also has the advantage of requiring less land usage than traditional farms. Some of these projects actually involve floating farms — theoretically, coastal cities could have far greater access to fresh, wholesome food in the future: One of the great health crises in American culture, today, is the lack of superior health food for the poor. It's encouraging that he is investing in such an important project. Vertical farming is at a fledgling stage, but it's a natural fit for ranch-raised Jeff; it also dovetails well with his insistence on product delivery speed and quality.

The forever young project:

As American demographics gray toward having more elderly people than young people for the first time in its history, science is being driven by the consumer. Accordingly, Jeff has invested in biomedical research associated with preventing the diseases correlated with aging. Some scientists are ambitious enough to hope that they may someday be able to halt aging... perhaps even be able to reverse the cell degeneration that causes the process. So, they want to help move cells backward in time in terms of health— essentially aging in reverse. Their first project is to try to tackle osteoporosis. The current treatments are rudimentary at best. Often, just recommendations for pain management like ibuprofen. Further projects would involve addressing other common diseases of old age: diabetes, heart disease, Alzheimer's, cancer, etc. Promisingly, in studies performed on mice with their current tech both a bent spine and cataracts were preventable. It's a thrilling ambition.

Education:

Perhaps one of the most interesting of Jeff's investments is into pre-school education. The availability and cost associated with American schools have long been a deeply contentious and troubling issue. There is also the tug-of-war over resource investment priorities— basically, which kids do you put special funds into? Do you address the needs of those that might fall behind without special attention, while leaving advanced students unchallenged? Or do you throw money toward gifted students at the cost of others? Theoretically, the oak tree, long-term version of Jeff's education ambitions will supply a round, tailored education to both parties. It is the hope that Jeff's new Day One program (still literally in its infancy— it caters to pre-school aged children) could give an education that is adapted to the needs of every single school-age child. What an impossibly natural fit for a student that excelled in his gifted program— for Jeff to use his educational opportunities to revolutionize a personal mold education model.

That means, children that learn best using their hands could be catered to, while also attending to children that are visual learners. Amazon's vast audible collection is ready-made for the needs of children that learn through listening. Watching education become as affordable and customer-centric as Jeff has made buying windshield wipers to the general public would be a beautiful investment into the next generation. Amazon's connections with over seventy countries also give it a unique position to provide affordable education on a globalized scale.

For example, in India there are the "lantern children". One enterprising teacher got funds for solar-powered lights that can be hung up in backpacks to charge during the day. Students, who are among some of the poorest in the world, finish work at factories to learn with him at night by the light of their solar lanterns. Jeff's commodification and adaptive business model could greatly aid efforts of this nature — India has hundreds of dialects; the commodification and diversification of textbook availability could aid this struggling democracy to rise.

Conclusion: The Life of Jeff Bezos

Ad astra per aspera is the Latin term for "to the stars through difficulty." Jeff Bezos has lived a life so rare as to be able to claim this expression. Jeff has aimed for and conquered the stars in a very literal sense while overcoming great odds. Jeff watched Neil Armstrong's descent down the ladder of the Apollo 11 spacecraft to the moon— and he knew, at the age of five, that someday the ladder of the space race would be his inheritance, his to climb. Despite economic challenges as a child, through his college disappointment over becoming a physicist, the risk of leaving Wall Street, and the chilly garage startup once upon a time. Jeff climbed from blueprints spread on desks made of doors, up from ruthless competitors, up through the dotcom bust, the failed inventions and the lost funds. In darkness and through doubt Jeff has climbed. And upon reaching the stars, Jeff used their nova to light the way to further, higher constellations of learning and success.
He used the light of Amazon to strike up Kindle books, which burst into Kindle Fire, which Echoed through American culture. He used their light to shine the way for agrarian science, health advancements, and education for children. Jeff

can say with Abraham Lincoln that he has well-withstood the tests of both adversity and power. May he find that when he looks back, that he sees earth by the starlight, may he rejoice that his blue origin is a better place for having known him.

Thank you for making it through to the end of *Jeff Bezos: An Extraordinary Life*. Let's hope it was informative and able to provide you with all of the tools you need to achieve your goals whatever they may be.

Finally, if you found this book useful in any way, a review on Amazon is always appreciated!

Printed in Great Britain
by Amazon